THE
INNER LIFE OF THE HOUSE OF COMMONS

THE INNER LIFE

OF THE

HOUSE OF COMMONS

BY

WILLIAM WHITE

Edited with a Preface by

JUSTIN MᶜCARTHY

AND WITH AN INTRODUCTION BY THE AUTHOR'S SON

VOL. I

BOOKS FOR LIBRARIES PRESS
FREEPORT, NEW YORK

100250

First Published 1897
Reprinted 1970

STANDARD BOOK NUMBER:
8369-5392-4

LIBRARY OF CONGRESS CATALOG CARD NUMBER:
79-119949

PRINTED IN THE UNITED STATES OF AMERICA

PREFACE.

IT has been a labour of love to me—one must use these old familiar phrases sometimes for the better expression of one's meaning—to go over these records which Mr. White has left to the public. My own recollections of the House of Commons extend over a great part of the time which is covered by Mr. White's descriptions of Parliamentary life. I first attended the House as a reporter in the Press Gallery at the opening of the Session of 1860. But I had often before that time as a young man visiting London found an opportunity of hearing a debate in the House of Lords and in the House of Commons. I have a clear recollection of all the principal figures which Mr. White describes. I remember Brougham well, and had some slight personal acquaintance with him. I remember Lord Lyndhurst and, of course, I remember Lord Palmerston. I do not remember Sir Robert Peel—the great Sir Robert Peel. He died before I ever saw London. But for the most part while reading through Mr. White's columns I found myself in an assemblage of familiar forms. My own impressions of the men whom Mr. White describes are, with very few exceptions, entirely in accordance with the estimate he makes and with the picture he paints.

One of these exceptions I make in the case of the late Sir

George Cornewall Lewis. My impression of Sir George
Lewis is that he was one of the very ablest men of his time
in Parliament. Mr. White does not seem to give him any
credit for humour. I think he had a marvellous gift of keen
and ready humour, a curious combination of wit, satire, and
common sense. I have heard it said by a long-experienced
Member of Parliament that Sir George Lewis delivered the
best speeches with the worst manner known to the House
of Commons of his time. I have written elsewhere that Sir
George Lewis began each of his speeches " by being nearly
inaudible, and continued to the last to be oppressed by the
most ineffective and unattractive manner and delivery."
But, I quote myself again, " it began to be gradually found
out that the monotonous, halting, feeble manner covered a
very remarkable power of expression ; that the speaker had
great resources of argument, humour, and illustration ; that
every sentence contained some fresh idea or some happy
phrase." " One who had watched parliamentary life
from without and within for many years said he had never
had his deliberate opinion changed by a speech in the
House of Commons but twice, and each time it was an
argument from Sir George Lewis that accomplished the
conversion." I think I can understand and explain the
difference of opinion between Mr. White and myself on the
subject of Sir George Lewis's capacity for debate. I fancy
that I had a much better opportunity of hearing Sir George
Lewis than that which his official occupation allowed to Mr.
White. I sat in the front row of the Reporters' Gallery,
just over Sir George Lewis's head, and after he had spoken
a sentence or two I could hear without effort or strain every
word that came from his lips. Therefore his most delicate
turns of humorous expression, his happiest touches of
literary illustration, were followed by me with ease and
enjoyment. I quite understand how different must be the

case of a listener who is stationed so far off that he loses half what the speaker is saying, and hears the other half only with difficulty and doubt, and misses the connection between one sentence and another. Men who listen nightly to the parliamentary debates do not as a rule follow closely every morning the reports in the newspapers. Therefore I can thoroughly understand Mr. White's lack of appreciation of Sir George Lewis as a parliamentary debater. What might not such a man have done in the House of Commons if he only had the voice and the articulation of Mr. Gladstone or Mr. Bright or Mr. Disraeli? A curious illustration of the difference between the effect of words according to their delivery is told in a parliamentary anecdote which I believe to be perfectly true. Early in the 'Sixties there was a great debate on foreign policy, chiefly relating to the cession of Nice and Savoy to France, in which Mr. Kinglake, the author of "Eothen," took a prominent part. Mr. Kinglake's speech was full of interest, and had, as might be expected, a literary beauty all its own. It closed with a remarkably eloquent and brilliant peroration, but unfortunately Mr. Kinglake had a thin and feeble voice, and very poor articulation. Most of the speech fell perfectly flat on the ear of the House of Commons. The House of Commons as a rule will not be induced to strain its attention to any speech unless it be a Budget speech of the Chancellor of the Exchequer, or some important Ministerial statement on foreign policy. Therefore the great majority of Members soon dropped Mr. Kinglake out of notice altogether, and his fine concluding sentences were absolutely thrown away. The late Sir Robert Peel intended to speak in the same debate. He was very much of Mr. Kinglake's views on the subject, and was greatly taken by Mr. Kinglake's peroration, which he was near enough to hear, while also quite conscious that it was utterly lost on the House. A bright idea occurred to him. He asked Mr. Kinglake if he might himself deliver the peroration which Kinglake had failed to make impressive. The author of " Eothen " indulged in no hallucination with regard to his effectiveness as a parliamentary orator, and he most willingly and good-humouredly granted the request. Sir Robert Peel spoke in the following night of the debate, and he wound up with Mr. Kinglake's peroration. But if that peroration could have had life and sense and hearing, what a difference it would have found in the manner of its reception! Sir Robert Peel, as we all remember, had a commanding presence, a splendid declamatory power, and a magnificent voice, capable of all variety of intonation and expression. He brought the House down, if we may use that phrase, with the sentences which, delivered by their real author the night before, had fallen dead upon the audience.

I presume that is an explanation of the difference of opinion between Mr. White and myself with regard to the parliamentary speeches of Sir George Lewis. I was so placed as to be able to hear all, or very nearly all, while Mr. White's official duties kept him rather out of range. With his descriptions of Palmerston, Lord John Russell, Gladstone, Cobden, and Bright, and even Sir Edward Bulwer-Lytton, I thoroughly agree. I say, even Sir Edward Bulwer-Lytton, because about him there was a great difference of opinion among listeners of the more critical order. He too suffered under some terrible disadvantages of voice and articulation. Until your ear grew a little accustomed to his way of speaking, it was sometimes impossible to understand him. But he had, at all events, a loud, strong voice, and when you had mastered his intonation you had no difficulty in following the speech. Now I am perfectly satisfied in my own mind that Sir Edward Bulwer-Lytton was not a great orator in the higher sense.

I am also satisfied that he was not a great novelist in the higher sense. But I know that, whatever criticism and satire might have said, the novels did take a tremendous grip of the reading public, and I know too that the speeches took a tremendous grip of the House of Commons. The speeches, no doubt, were often flashy; the arguments were very often sham which could have satisfied no creature; but the "phrasing" was superb, and phrasing goes a long way with the House of Commons. You might try to analyse away as long as you chose the reality and the merit of Sir Edward Bulwer-Lytton's success as a speaker, but you could not reason away the fact that he was for the time a great success, and that he crowded and held the House of Commons in a manner never surpassed by any parliamentary orator within my recollection. Let us admit, if you will, that the effect was evanescent, and that nobody now would think of comparing Sir Edward Bulwer-Lytton as a parliamentary speaker with Mr. Gladstone or Mr. Cobden, or Mr. Bright or Mr. Disraeli. He was the comet of a season, as in later days was Mr. Robert Lowe. But the comet of a season at all events has his season, and we cannot deny that he blazed in his time. I have been much interested in Mr. White's appreciation of Sir Edward Bulwer-Lytton. Like myself, he is evidently puzzled as to the reasons and the merits of the success; but, like myself, too, he sees that the success was there and makes no effort to deny it.

I thoroughly agree in Mr. White's opinions also with regard to another man of quite a different order—Mr. John Stuart Mill. Nine out of every ten people would have told you at the time that Mr. Mill was a dead failure in the House of Commons. Mr. White was of quite a different opinion. So was I at the time, and so am I now. As Mr. White points out, you have to ask yourself when con-

sidering whether a man was a failure or a success, what
you think the man set before himself to do. If Mr. Mill
had gone into the House of Commons with an ambition to
make rattling, declamatory speeches which would call forth
salvoes of applause from one side and indignant protes-
tations from the other, then, indeed, we should have to admit
that he had not realised his ambition, and, in fact, that he
was an absolute failure. But Mr. Mill went into the House
of Commons for no such purpose. If you had foolishly tried
to flatter him by telling him that he had all the qualities
of a great parliamentary orator he would have smiled with
a benignant, pitying smile, and waved the whole subject
away. He went into Parliament at a peculiar time, when
some great public questions were stirring on which it was
felt that he could speak with influence and with authority,
and that he could lift the debate above the level of ordinary
partisan controversy. On this account he was pressed to go
into the House of Commons, and on this account he consented to undertake the task just as he would have consented to undertake any task to which it was shown him
that his duty called him. He accomplished his purpose.
More than once he turned the whole debate into the right
channel. Many of his phrases still vibrate in the memory
of the House, and are quoted again and again by people who
have forgotten to whom the phrases owe their authorship.
The curious half-poetic yet wholly truthful reply to the
cynical question, as to what posterity has done for us,
showing that posterity, by our natural longing to have its
approval, has stimulated most of the brave deeds done in
the world, enthralled the House of Commons by its literary
charm and its exalted purpose. I am glad to find myself in
such absolute accord as to Mill's parliamentary career with
so keen and sure an observer as Mr. White, a man to whom
it mattered nothing whether a speaker rose on this side of

the House or on that, and who was as full of admiration
for genuine success as he was full of contempt for quackery
and sham, and of kindly mercy to commonplace mediocrity.

No finer or truer study of Cobden can be found anywhere
than is found in Mr. White's columns. I speak of Mr.
Cobden especially because his presence is no longer as fresh
in public recollection as it was a quarter of a century ago.
Gladstone we have still with us, and Bright has not very
long left us, and even young men can remember Disraeli's
parliamentary presence and style and methods. But
Cobden passed from among us more than thirty years
ago, and the younger generation cannot know of its
own knowledge anything about his style as a parliamentary
orator and debater. Richard Cobden's name and services
will never be forgotten in our history, but Mr. White
enables younger readers to do what they might not otherwise be able to do—to see the man in his habit as he lived.
Mr. White's are living pictures indeed. The world would
be ever so much the richer if only we could have had some
such descriptions of the House of Commons in the days of
Pitt and Fox and Burke and Sheridan—in the days of
Bolingbroke and Walpole and Pulteney.

I have not made any attempt at the arrangement of these
descriptive records with a view to the presentation of a
sort of historical diary of events as they occurred in Parliament. Of course I have preserved the natural sequence of
dates, and no description is taken out of its time and its
order of succession. What I mean is that I have altogether abandoned the idea of giving anything like an equal
share of space to each succeeding week or month or
measure. A parliamentary diary would have many uses,
quite apart from what Hansard and the journals of the
two Houses can do for us, but Mr. White's work would
be thrown away upon a mere parliamentary diary, even if

the amount of space its contents must occupy did not make
it impossible as a book for popular reading.   Therefore I
have sometimes left days and weeks of parliamentary work
quite unrecorded and without description.   Mr. White had
to write his weekly contribution to the illustrated paper
with which he was connected, and each week's topics were
living and interesting then.   Now we have to adopt a
totally different principle of arrangement in accordance with
the changed perspective.   Many measures were passed in
each session which greatly interested the public then, but
are of little concern now even to students of parliamentary
history.   I have always therefore picked out the subjects
which have still an interest for the public, and so endeavoured to help the public to understand how and by whom
these questions were debated at the time.

I have endeavoured not to burden my readers with too
much explanation.   Sometimes—as, for example, in the case
of the debate on the evacuation of Kars—I have thought
it necessary to give a short statement as to the whole
subject of controversy.   I have had to do this in other
instances as well.   But where a debate seems capable of
telling its own story I have allowed its own tale to be
enough even for the youngest of readers.   Some of my
difficulty with regard to the inclusion of this debate and
the exclusion of that other lay in the fact that I found
myself rather apt, occasionally, to confound my own
personal interest in a parliamentary controversy with the
probable interest of the reader of this day.   Perhaps I
had listened to the whole controversy and it lived freshly
in my memory; and yet it may have been a matter of
no abiding interest whatever, and not in the least worth
the study of busy human beings in the world of to-day.
As with the controversies, so, too, with the controversialists.
There were men thirty years ago, to stretch no farther back,

who managed for the time to engage the attention of the public, and who seem to be now as forgotten as the hobby-horse itself was in Hamlet's time. I have not thought it worth while to endeavour to revivify, through Mr. White's descriptions, these out-lived reputations. Where there was anything odd, or droll, or fantastic—and such curious phenomena have been seen in most parliamentary generations —I have usually allowed Mr. White to give us his ideas about them. I have been particular, in many cases, to preserve his description of any new member who in his maiden speech gave promise of real future success. Readers who go through these volumes will be surprised and pleased to find how often Mr. White foresaw what was in a man destined to rise, and told his readers, if I may say so, to "watch that square" and look out for a coming success. Some of the then young men whose maiden speeches he criticised and applauded have grown elderly gentlemen, or old gentlemen, by this time; and some have given up parliament altogether—and some have given up life. But it is interesting to find in the pages of these volumes how many a time Mr. White has anticipated the final judgment of parliament and of the public. It has to be remembered, too, as Mr. White himself points out, that it is very hard to judge one way or the other by a maiden speech. Many a man has made a highly successful maiden speech and never made a speech worth listening to after. Many a man, on the other hand, has made an utter failure with his maiden speech—as Sheridan did, and as Disraeli did—who afterwards took a place in the very front rank of parliamentary debate. Mr. Gladstone's maiden speech fell so utterly unnoticed that, until some recent publications had settled the question, he was almost invariably set down as having made his first speech at a later date, and on a more important subject. All the greater credit, therefore, must

we give to Mr. White for having so often got the right
appreciation, and so seldom missed it. " Sir," says Lucius,
in "Cymbeline", "the event is yet to name the winner." But
this is exactly what one cannot often do who has to describe a
maiden speech ; for the delivery of a maiden speech, successful
or otherwise, does not by any means name the winner. Mr.
White has all the honour of having several times named the
winner before the decisive event.

Not many very important changes have been made in the
rules or the ways of the House of Commons since the time
when Mr. White was describing parliamentary life. Still
there have been some changes which deserve a notice.
Amongst these are the alterations in the rules of the
House, which have for their object the control and
limitation of debate. The House of Commons is always
overstocked with business, and at one time an absolute
and unlimited freedom of discussion was allowed. Of
late years the defect of such a system was made especially
evident by the results of the obstruction which the Irish
Nationalist members started with a distinct purpose of
their own. Obstruction had always been a recognised
instrument in parliamentary controversy. The Reform
Bill of Lord Grey and Lord John Russell was obstructed
in the House of Commons at every stage. There was a
Committee appointed by the Tory members, of which Sir
Robert Peel himself was the Chairman, to make arrangements for systematic obstruction. Mr. Gladstone obstructed
the Divorce Bill to the best of his extraordinary capacity.
Sir John Pope Hennessy, acting under the direct authority
and inspiration of Mr. Disraeli, kept the House sitting for
nearly all night on many occasions. Sir Charles Dilke and
some of his friends kept on debating and dividing more than
once, until even the sun of winter shone in through the
painted windows of the House of Commons. No attempt,

however, was made to limit the length of debate during all
this time. In every single instance the obstruction was
directed to one particular measure, and everybody knew
that when that particular measure had been disposed of
in one way or the other, the obstruction would come to
an end. It was therefore not thought worth while to
introduce any new rules for the purpose of getting rid
of a merely casual and temporary difficulty. But Irish
obstruction was a totally different thing. Its aim was to
insist that if the House of Commons would not give its
attention to the Irish National claims and the Irish
agricultural grievances, the House should not be allowed
to go on with any other business. Now, it is not for
me to offer any opinion as to the justification of such a
policy. To me, of course, it must have seemed to be
justifiable, for otherwise I never could have taken part
in it. But it is certain that it turned the attention of
Parliament to the necessity for taking some measures to
limit the length of debate.

One of the measures was that which Mr. Gladstone
described as the devolution of business. Two Grand
Committees were formed, one on law and one on trade,
to which various measures might be referred after they
had passed the second reading, and where the Committee
stage could be got through much more satisfactorily than
in the House itself. This has proved to be on the whole
an excellent arrangement; but it would not of itself have
had much effect in the way of shortening debate in the
House when there was any strong motive for prolonging
it. Therefore a number of new rules were passed at
different times, introducing the principle of closure and
giving the leader of the House and the Speaker greater
power of dealing with irrelevant or manifestly obstructive
debate. Even still it seems to most persons that there

is room for yet further restriction. Everybody knows
that the House of Commons is afflicted with the presence
of a number of what I may call professional talkers and
professional bores, who have not the Irish party's excuse for
obstruction, who have nothing to say that any one cares to
hear, who have no experience to contribute which could be
of the slightest use to the House and to whom nobody
listens. Some of these gentlemen speak on every question
brought before the House, and when they speak at all they
speak at portentous length. Now I do not know why some
reasonable rule might not be adopted which would set a
certain limit to speeches in general, making an exception,
of course, in the case of Ministerial expositions of policy,
of replies from the leaders of Opposition, and of speeches
delivered in moving or opposing the second reading of
important measures. At present, however, I am only
concerned to say that certain changes have taken place
in the rules of the House of Commons since Mr. White's
time, and that these are likely to be the precursors of other
changes in the future.

The rules which regulate admission to the inner lobby
have also been greatly altered. At one time everybody
might pass through Westminster Hall and St. Stephen's
Hall and through the outer lobby to the inner lobby
without, as a rule, being challenged by anybody. If by
chance some policeman stopped the visitor and asked him
what his business was, the visitor had only to say that
he wished to see a certain member of the House and
mention the member's name, and he was then admitted
as a matter of course. It used to be a great delight to
me when a very young man, on a visit to London, thus
to enter the inner lobby and see Lord Palmerston, or
Lord John Russell, or Mr. Cobden, or Mr. Bright come
out from the House and talk to his friends. At that

time too the inner lobby was hardly ever overcrowded.
As anybody could go in there, few people really wanted
to go in. Charles Lever's Mrs. Dodd lays it down as a
principle of social life that nobody wants to go anywhere
unless he or she is assured that there is no human
possibility of getting in. Now that the entrance to the
inner lobby is rigidly guarded by all manner of restrictions,
that lobby is often overcrowded, almost to suffocation.
Everybody wants to go in there, and a member can
always obtain permission for a constituent or any other
man who is a friend of his to pass through that lobby
and linger there a little in his company; and so the life
of the poor member is embittered by incessant applications
for the privilege. The restrictions were put on at the time
of the dynamite explosions. Up to that period any member
might issue orders for admission to the Strangers' Gallery
any night and every night. For a long time it was a question
of first come, first served, for the holders of orders; afterwards it was the custom that those who held orders should
ballot for precedence. Obviously, this system relieved a
member of all responsibility. He gave an order to anybody who asked for it; it was no affair of his whether
the holder of the order succeeded or failed in finding a
place in the Gallery. But when the dynamite crisis was
on, it was thought necessary that some check should be
placed on the issue of orders, and some responsibility
attached to it. Now, therefore, a member has to ask for
an order, either from the Speaker's secretary or from the
Sergeant-at-Arms or, in certain cases, from the Speaker himself. Some change was, under all conditions, reasonable and
even necessary. But, curiously enough, it was left free to
every member to introduce any number of ladies into the
inner lobby without asking the permission of the Speaker or
the Sergeant or any one else. Every member in the course

of a session introduces to the inner lobby a number of ladies whom he never saw or heard of in his life before. Perhaps they are from his constituency; perhaps they are strangers who merely send in their cards. It is not much trouble to bring them in, and most members are courteous enough to undertake the duty. If a friend and his wife and daughters come to ask any member for admission to the inner lobby, the member may bring in the friend's wife and daughters without asking any one's permission, but for the friend himself, whom perhaps he has known since his boyhood, he must get a " pink ticket " of admission from the Sergeant-at-Arms. Now I am considering all this for the moment in its reference to the dynamite crisis. Why should there be more danger of dynamite in my introduction of an old and intimate friend to the inner lobby than in my introduction of half a dozen ladies from, let us say, Chicago or New Orleans, whom I had never seen or heard of before, and who, for aught I know, may be carrying neatly done up packets of dynamite under their skirts?

In Mr. White's days, too, the institution of tea on the Terrace in the early summer was practically unknown. If he were living now it would much amaze him to see the Terrace at certain hours on every day in the summer covered almost all over by crowds of ladies treated by their friends in Parliament to tea and strawberries, and waited on by attendant girls. One evening a session or two ago, a beautiful summer evening, while the Terrace was thus crowded, an excursion steamer going up the river thronged with people passed close by our river wall. Every eye in the steamer was turned on our festive gathering, and at last a stentorian voice from the steamer's deck cried out, " Why don't ye go into the 'Ouse of Commons and do your business?" Some of us might have explained to him, if time allowed, that perhaps the best chance of getting our business done was for as many members as possible to sit on the Terrace and abstain from the House. Mr. White would be astonished if he could see the inner lobby literally crammed, as it often is now during summer months, with ladies from all parts of the world who are invited to have tea on the Terrace, and who, meanwhile, linger longer in the lobby to see what is going on. Still more surprised would he be, perhaps, if he could see what happens very often on those Terrace evenings when the division-bell suddenly rings. Then every member jumps up and makes for the one available staircase—a narrow, twisted, and darksome ascent. Down this same staircase a stream of ladies is pouring; most of these ladies have not the faintest notion why members should come rushing like madmen up the stairs, and they never think of flattening themselves against the wall or the balustrade to allow the struggling members to get to their division-lobby. I am not finding any fault with this free admission of ladies. I should be very sorry to curtail their privilege of entrance or entertainment. Only I think it might be as well to construct another staircase or two, which should be sacred to the upward flight of members summoned by the suddenly-ending, shrilly voice of the division-bell.

At all events, it seems to me a matter of much interest that here at least, if he could live again, Mr. White, with all his parliamentary experience, would find something to surprise him.

INTRODUCTION.

WILLIAM WHITE was born at Bedford in the year 1807. He was educated at the Grammar School, and for many years was a bookseller in the town. He was also one of the trustees of the schools, and it was mainly through his efforts that this great institution did not become sectarian. For this service his friends presented him with a handsome testimonial. In 1854 he was appointed by Lord Charles Russell assistant-doorkeeper to the House of Commons, and soon afterwards became doorkeeper. It then occurred to him that something might be done to make the Parliamentary debates more interesting, and a series of sketches, published originally in the *Illustrated Times*, was the result. Nowadays these descriptive reports are common enough, but in 1855 the idea was new. They are written in pure, idiomatic English, and not only do they represent the transactions in the House with a pictorial fidelity which is unattainable by the ordinary "graphic" style, but they frequently supply a key to much that happened which, without them, would be unintelligible. They are therefore a real contribution to the history of the times. Naturally they brought him into friendly relationships with many members of the House. They valued his judgments on political matters, but the oracles he consulted were simply the plain integrity and common sense which were his guide in private life. It may be mentioned, by the way, that he was an admirable public speaker, never wasting his words, never attempting to delude his audience by an easy attack on weak points which were unessential and by neglecting what was central and important, but always going straight to the heart of the controversy. He was a student of the best English literature, and occasionally lectured on literary subjects. When he did so, it was apparent that, underneath the simplicity and directness which externally were his most obvious characteristics, there lay imagination and a singular capacity for being moved by that which is genuinely sublime in Nature and Art.

He retired in 1875, and a hundred members of the House united to testify their "high appreciation" of him by a most generous gift.

In 1882 he died, and was buried at Carshalton, where he was then living.

Thanks are due to the present proprietors of the *Illustrated London News* for permission to collect and publish the "Inner Life."

W. H. W.

CONTENTS.

CHAPTER VIII.

CHAPTER IX.

CHAPTER X.

CHAPTER XI.

CHAPTER XII.

CHAPTER XIII.

CHAPTER XIV.

CHAPTER XV.

CHAPTER XVI.

CHAPTER XVII.

CHAPTER I.

LORD PALMERSTON—MR. HAYTER—MR. DISRAELI : IN THE
LOBBY—SIR EDWARD BULWER-LYTTON.

Mar. 8, 1856.* LORD PALMERSTON is "the foremost man in all the House." Strangers who enter the House for the first time generally ask, "Which is the Premier?" and especially is this the case with foreigners— no sooner are they seated but they cast about for some one to show them *Palmerestong.* Those strangers who cannot get into the House, and who wish to see the Noble Lord, should place themselves in the lobby. About five o'clock any day, when the House sits, he may be seen crossing from the members' staircase to the House ; but the strangers must keep a sharp look out, or he will be gone before they catch a glimpse of him—for the grass never grows near the feet of the Noble Lord—he always moves at a quick pace. When he arrives at the door his messenger, waiting there, hands him his despatch-box ; he then swings through the door, and passing along the left division-lobby enters the House at the back of the Speaker's chair, and takes his seat about the middle of the Treasury Bench ; and there he sits with his hat on, his face in deep shadow, looking as if he

* The marginal dates throughout this work are those of the various issues of the *Illustrated Times,* from which the editor's selection has been made.

were fast asleep through the whole of the sitting, excepting for about half an hour, when he adjourns to the refreshment rooms, or when he rises to address the House. But, as the proverb says, " Catch a weasel asleep "; the Hon. Member who may fancy that the Noble Lord is napping, and takes the opportunity to say something smart touching his Lordship, will certainly very soon discover his mistake. We believe the Noble Lord seldom sleeps in the House, and when he does he sleeps as the cats are said to do when they watch at a mouse-hole.

Lord Palmerston is, we should say, about five feet ten inches in height, looks about fifty-five years old—not more, albeit he is turned seventy—walks upright as a dart, and steps out like a soldier. He always, in the House, wears a surtout coat, buttoned up close, dark trousers, and black necktie. His Lordship does not affect preciseness or fashion in dress, like his opponent Disraeli, or his colleague Mr. Vernon Smith. We have seen Cabinet Ministers frequently in full dress on the Treasury Bench, but Palmerston never. Indeed, from the opening of the Parliament to the prorogation, he seems to us to eschew all pleasure, sticking to the House as a diligent tradesman sticks to his shop. Further, after the day's labour, even though the House sat far into the morning, we have heard that he generally walks home. We passed him ourselves one morning, in broad daylight, last session, in Parliament Street; he was chatting away as briskly as if he had freshly risen from his bed; and yet that day there had been a morning sitting, and he was in his seat soon after one p.m., and then it was past two a.m.

Lord Palmerston is not an orator—at least, not of the old school. He never attempts lofty eloquence; but he is a clear and effective speaker, and very sagacious; long experience, of course, has made him so. He not only knows exactly what to say, but what also to leave unsaid. And, of course, he is always listened to with profound attention, not merely because he speaks as one having authority, but also on account of his great talents, long official career, and boundless knowledge. When some men, even some Ministers, rise there is a rush of Members to the door; but if it is announced in the lobby, or in the dining-room, on an important night, that "Pam." is up, the House is filled as if by magic.

A good deal has been said about the joking propensities of the Premier—far more than is due. The fact is, that the Noble Lord, considering the number of speeches which he makes, does not often launch a joke, and never, whatsoever may be said to the contrary, on a serious subject. When he indulges in wit, it is in return for some wit that has been thrown at him, and frequently those who have been the losers at this game have been the men to preach seriousness to their Noble Opponent. Mr. Bright used often to allude to the Premier's levity, but we imagine he will not soon do it again; for the last lecture on this topic which he delivered was met by such a happy retort that the House was convulsed with laughter, in which the Hon. Member for Manchester himself could not help joining. Mr. Bright, during a long speech, had scolded the Premier for his witty sallies and general levity; but quite forgetting to apply his sermon to himself, he had tried his hand at some rather ponderous jokes. In reply the Noble Lord said, "The Hon. Member has taken me to task for what he is pleased to call my levity. Now, it is rather remarkable that in the Hon. Member's speech there were no less than ten jokes. I cannot, however, find fault with the levity of these jokes, for there was no *levity* in them." One peculiarity of Lord Palmerston's wit ought not to be unnoticed—it seldom, if ever, wounds. Indeed, the very man against whom it is directed may often be heard joining in the general chorus of laughter, and the Premier himself laughs also—and laughs heartily, too. There is this marked difference between him and his opponent Disraeli : Palmerston's witty sallies are evidently suggested by a love of fun, quite as much as by a desire to hit an opponent; Disraeli's shafts are too frequently hurled with a spiteful intent. Palmerston laughs with genuine merriment; Disraeli seldom or never laughs, either at his own or others' jokes—unless a sardonic curl of the lip or the faintest ray of a smile may be called a laugh.

Mar. 15, 1856. Who is the most powerful member of the House of Commons ? Lord Palmerston ? No ! Mr. Disraeli ? By no means. The most powerful member of the House is unquestionably the Right Hon. William Goodenough Hayter, member for Wells, and " Whipper-in " for Government. Palmerston and Disraeli make long speeches. Mr. Hayter flourishes figuratively a long and formidable whip—and the whip is very much more effective than the most eloquent harangues. A good speech may possibly change the mind of some two or three members during a debate, but Mr. Hayter, by his more effective logic, brings up scores of sluggish members to the division. The House of Commons is the most talkative assembly in the world; but victories there are not achieved by talk. Does the reader doubt this ? Let him, then, note the fact that, on an average, not more than one-half of the members whose names appear on the division-list ever hear the debate. Just as at an election success does not, as old electioneers well know, depend upon pot-house orations or long addresses, but upon organisation, the activity of the Committee and the scouts, so Ministerial measures are seldom carried by oratory, but by the zeal, foresight, and energy of the " Whip."

On the occasion of the late Church-rate debate we met in the lobby a Dissenting agitator against this obnoxious impost. "Well," said we, "how goes the war? Shall you win or lose?" "Doubtful!" was the reply. But we soon saw that it was not doubtful, for, after we had been in the lobby a short time, we observed some significant movement which, to a practised eye, was decisive. The fact was, that Government had determined to support the measure, and Messrs. Hayter and Co. were busy whipping for a division. And the result proved the correctness of our conclusions, for the Bill was carried through the second reading by a majority of 43, albeit some 40 or 50 Church-rate opponents were away.

Strangers who wish to see Disraeli must take their stand in the lobby on any night when a party debate of consequence is expected to come off; and between four and five p.m. let them place themselves by the side of some friend who knows him, or some communicative policeman. He comes up the members' private staircase, marches across the lobby, solemnly and slowly, generally alone, and speaking to no one as he passes. On his arrival at the door of the House he always casts an upward glance at the clock, passes into the division-lobby, takes off his hat, goes round to the back of the Speaker's chair, then to his seat, and carefully stows his hat under the bench. He then sits down, folds his arms across his breast, and keeps immovably in this position, with his eyes fixed upon the ground, until he rises to speak.

April 5, 1856. It is a peculiarity of Disraeli that he never wears his hat in the House. Most of the members sit covered, as well as Government officials. It is convenient for them to do so. The hat is a kind of pent-house under which they can retire from the gaze of the members and of strangers ; for as the light comes all from the ceiling the brim of the hat throws the upper part of the face into shadow ; and whether they wince under an attack or are excited to a smile, nobody can see their movements. But Disraeli needs no hat, for he neither winces nor laughs, and seldom cheers ; in fact, he sits like an imperturbable statue. His place is between Napier and Walpole or Whiteside, but he seldom speaks to his neighbours. Though in the midst of his party, he appears not to be of them, but is as separate and distinct as his race is from all the world. Sometimes he goes into the division-lobby or a private room to consult with his colleagues in opposition, but seldom to gossip. Last session, indeed, the wondering members, as they passed one of the recesses in the division-lobby, saw the Right Hon. Leader of her Majesty's Opposition in close conversation with Mr. Bright ; and it was probably this circumstance reported to the editor of the *Morning Advertiser* that led that sagacious prophet to foretell a coalition between the sturdy Quaker and the Jew. But it turned out to be only one of those mare's nests which the " able editor " is so often discovering. What the Right Hon. and Hon. Members talked about it is impossible to say ; and whether they agreed, and if so, on what curious subject two such men could agree, must remain a secret. One thing is only known, that these two men did once sit together and talk about something for nearly an hour.

If strangers wish to hear Disraeli speak at any length and *no more*, they must be contented to wait in the gallery until eleven, twelve, or it may be one o'clock, for he seldom harangues until the close of the debate. He rather chooses to be last, after Lord Palmerston, but sometimes he is obliged to speak before the Noble Lord.

It is not uncommon for persons to be very much disappointed with Disraeli's speaking. They had heard a great deal about his oratorical powers, and they expected to hear lofty eloquence like that which, in classic times, " shook the arsenal and fulmined over Greece." It is as well, therefore, to inform all persons who have not been to the House that we have no such oratory there—nothing of the sort. The last of the orators was Harry Brougham, and when he consented to place his light under a coronet oratory in the House of Commons became extinct. Disraeli can talk well, can be pungent, biting, witty. Gladstone can pour out words by the hour together—a perennial stream of words, and can reason closely. Cobden, when in right order, and on a right subject, can deal logical blows —these will shiver a fallacy to dust. Palmerston speaks as one having authority, and can speak well, too ; and many others can also talk reasonably well. But none are orators of the old type. None can loftily declaim or utter grand and abiding truths with that energy, force, and passion which startle the hearers, and make even opponents cheer against their will. Disraeli is a good speaker, according to the modern House of Commons gauge, but he is not a great orator.

When he rises he generally starts bolt upright, then leans his hands upon the table, and casts his eyes downwards. At first he not infrequently hesitates and stammers a good deal, shambling like an old mail-coach horse who has got stiff by standing in the stall, but, like the said coach-horse, he soon warms up to his work. He then takes his hands off the table, thrusts them it may be into his waistcoat-pocket, and turns his face towards the House ; or else, if he feels well up, he folds his arms across his breast. Then he hesitates no more, but his sentences come out in stately flow. Disraeli's sentences are specially remark-able for their excellent English, and for the peculiar

appropriateness of his words, especially of his adjectives.
If there is an adjective in the language specially suitable
to express his meaning, that he will be sure to use. But
still he generally disappoints, for the first three-quarters
of an hour, strangers who hear him for the first time.
There is nothing witty, nothing specially brilliant, for it
is his peculiarity that he reserves all his wit and brilliancy
until he is about to finish ; and those who are used to him
well know when it is coming. He shifts his position, turning
with his face towards the Treasury Bench, and heralds the
coming witticism by a slight curl of the mouth and twinkle
of the eyes. And then for about a quarter of an hour, if
he be quite himself and the occasion is favourable, it is
seen that he still possesses that power of sarcasm and wit
which so galled Sir Robert Peel in the Corn Law struggle.

April 12, 1856. We have before said, or ought to have said,
that the lobby of the House is the best place
in the world to see the world's notabilities. No foreigner,
of course, comes to England during the session without
paying a visit to the House of Commons ; and everybody
in England—whether " known to fame " or " born to blush
unseen "—will like to see the House and hear the debates,
sometime during his life, or probably have some business to
transact with one or other of the members. A constant
attendance, therefore, in the lobby will be sure to bring
you into contact with all sorts of people. The officers and
policemen in the lobby probably have seen as many celebrities in their time as the Premier. Not long ago we were
lounging in this place when we were startled by hearing the
name of Rawlinson, and, on inquiry, we found that the tall,
handsome man with the moustache, who had for some
time been pacing up and down with Mr. Danby Seymour
was the learned Orientalist, whose name is as familiar to

every reader of Eastern travels as household words. At another time a magnificent-looking fellow, in Eastern costume—certainly one of the handsomest men we ever saw—entered upon the scene. His noble port and manly bearing attracted our attention at once—we were certain that he was "somebody"; and we soon discovered that he was an Afghan chief—one of those splendid cavalry officers whose prowess England has often had to acknowledge. The man was a study, and kept our eyes riveted for some time. It is by no means uncommon to see the Indian costume in the Ambassadors' Gallery, and very picturesque it looks there, contrasting with the plain and unrelieved dress of our senators. And so let us take our stand in the lobby again. We shall be sure to see somebody of greater or lesser note.

Here is one. Do you see that gigantic man in the centre, talking to a cluster of members, and overtopping all by head and shoulders? That is "Jacob Omnium" of the *Times*. His real name is Higgins. Some military matters are to be discussed to-night, and he has come to learn whether any of his suggestions are likely to be carried out. He will find no difficulty in getting under the gallery, and there he will sit below the bar, but having more real power, perhaps, over the decision than many that sit above it.

The tall gentleman with the silver hair is Mr. Dallas, the new American Minister. And there goes another celebrity. Do you see that strange-looking man with the bushy moustache, imperial, and aquiline nose? That is the famous novelist, Sir Edward George Earle Lytton Bulwer-Lytton. He certainly is, as you say, a very remarkable-looking man. He always walks about in that abstracted manner, rather stooping, his hat on the back of his head, his hands thrust into his trouser pockets, and his eyes cast downwards—looking for all the world as if he fancied that he had lost something, and was searching on the ground and feeling for it in his pockets at the same time. It is generally known about the House when he is going to speak, as he then wanders about more abstractedly than usual. The Hon. Baronet is not an effective speaker; not, however, because his matter is not good, but because his action spoils all. It is well known that he studies his speeches carefully beforehand—would that he would, under proper guidance, study how to deliver them! His manner is this: He begins a sentence, standing upright, in his usual tone; as he gets to the middle he throws himself backwards, until you would fancy that he must tumble over, and gradually raises his voice to its highest pitch. He then begins to lower his tone and bring his body forwards, so that at the finish of the sentence his head nearly touches his knees, and the climax of the sentence is lost in a whisper; and yet, notwithstanding this serious drawback, there are but few members whose speeches are comparable to Sir Edward's. Strange that a man who thinks it worth his while to get up his matter carefully should pay so little attention to his manner.

CHAPTER II.

[The fortress of Kars, in Armenia, held out against the Russians to the very close of the war. Kars was defended by Colonel Fenwick Williams, an English officer, afterwards Sir Fenwick Williams of Kars, who was sent out to re-organise the Turkish troops in Armenia after they had undergone a terrible defeat by the Russians. Kars, under Williams, held out so stubbornly and so splendidly that when it had to surrender to famine, the garrison was allowed to march out with all the honours of war. There was a strong conviction on the part of the Opposition that the surrender would never have taken place but for the want of foresight and of energy in the Government at home ; and Mr. Whiteside's motion was a vote of censure on that ground.]

May 10, 1856. WE have had an old-fashioned party-fight— such a fight as the House has not indulged itself with during this session—a crack debate, and more than 500 members in a division. The debate was opened by Mr. Whiteside, continued through three nights, and ended at 12.30 on the third, with a division giving 123 majority to her Majesty's Government.

Lord Palmerston has, in fact, stood a fierce siege, like

11

General Williams at Kars; with this difference—General Williams was neglected, failed to get money, provisions, and troops, and was at length obliged to surrender to the enemy. The Premier was not thus deserted, but, on the contrary, by skilful policy and the energetic zeal of his subalterns, men were brought up from all directions, and he won a splendid but an easy victory. Much of this was owing to his own generalship. That meeting of his in his own dining-room was a capital manœuvre, and it was there that he raised the enthusiasm of his followers and placed himself at their head. His "whips," too, were also on the alert. Circulars were sent to the four winds of heaven, every man of the party was summoned to his post, and the effect was, that though numbers were scattered in every direction, when the battle came no fewer than 303 good men and true divided with the Noble Lord, and gave to him a crushing majority.

Mr. Whiteside, the Hon. Member who led the attack, is an Irish barrister. He was for a short time, in 1852, Irish Solicitor-General when Lord Derby was Premier and Disraeli Chancellor of the Exchequer, and hopes to be so again, or something higher, in "the good time coming," when his friends shall again return to power. Hence his zeal for Williams and his country's honour. Mr. Whiteside in person is very tall and thin, partly bald-headed, has unusually long arms, rather stooping shoulders, and is, on the whole, a fine-looking man, though somewhat ungainly in his carriage. The Hon. Member is brother to the Rev. Dr. Whiteside, vicar of Scarborough, and the two brothers may often be seen walking together in the lobby—interesting studies, as each is a type of the class to which he belongs. Both are very tall, but the lawyer is pale, thin, and looks overworked, while the parson is portly, rubicund—a jolly specimen of a class of men who live well and work little. The Hon.

Member is said by his admirers to be a great man, and the
speech with which he opened the debate has been declared,
by no less an authority than Mr. Disraeli, to be equal to
anything that was delivered in the eighteenth century, when
Burke and Chatham were at the zenith of their fame. But
then it must be remembered that Disraeli spoke as a partisan,
and, moreover, is strongly suspected sometimes of indulging
in what is called *flamming*. That it was an extraordinary
speech cannot be questioned—it took more than four hours
to deliver it. It was passionate and fervid, as all Irishmen's
speeches are, and Mr. Whiteside's especially—sometimes,
indeed, quite volcanic—and was spoken with a physical
energy and extravagance of action that made the hearers
fear lest the speaker should break a blood-vessel or fall
down in a fit. But a great speech it was not—except upon
the principle that he is a great artist who uses a great brush.
Lord Palmerston happily and wittily described it as a speech
long to be remembered by all who *saw* it ; and a dry old
member who has been in the House for thirty years, in
answer to a question whether he did not greatly admire it,
said, in his usual quiet way, " It certainly was a remarkable
specimen of physical power." Mr. Whiteside always speaks
with passion, whether his subject is a vulgar road Bill or the
impeachment of a minister ; and yet in conversation and
private life the Hon. Member is quiet, amiable, and gentle-
manly. Out of the House he reminds us of a beautiful hill
covered over with greensward, and all the signs of peace ; in
the House he is the same hill—but grown volcanic.

With the exception of some four or five speeches the
debate was dull and vapid as spent soda-water. There was
a very large number of members " about," but they would
not stay in the House. When Mr. Whiteside began he
had an audience of some 300 members, but even his fiery
declamation could not keep them together, for in half an

hour at least 100 had gone away—some to dine, some to write their letters, and a goodly number to smoke and gossip below. The Hon. Member began at 5.20 and finished at 9.25 ; and it was amusing to see the surprise and dismay of Hon. Gentlemen when they returned, after three hours' or so absence, and found Mr. Whiteside still on his legs. " What, not down yet! why, he will speak for ever." One incident in the speech deserves to be recorded, as it was a cause of no little merriment to those who stopped. About 7.30 the Hon. Member delivered what seemed to be a very fervid peroration, and as it was confidently expected and hoped that the end was come, the members of the Opposition cheered long and vociferously ; but, lo ! instead of sitting down, as it was expected he would, the Hon. Member quietly said, " *And now to business !* " and the House found that all that had gone before was only preliminary; " the business " was yet to come. A shout of laughter broke from the Government side, and, indeed, from all parts of the House at this "sell." Time will, however, beat even an Irish lawyer at last, and at 9.25 the Hon. Member finished, and the House was all but deserted. And during all that night and the next, and part of the third, the debate " dragged its slow length along " in the most uninteresting, tiresome, and even painful manner. On the second night, as a division was confidently expected, the House was very full at 12 o'clock. But how the Noble Lord at the head of her Majesty's Government determined to finish the night, divided the House, gained a large majority, and subsequently, in the exuberance of his joy over his victory, graciously gave way, is all too well known to be dwelt upon here. On the third night the debate was duller than ever. Indeed, in the middle of the evening it really seemed as if the House would " faint away." When Mr. Liddell sat down there were exactly 35 Members present, and some minutes elapsed before any speaker would rise. And when Sir James Graham began the number had only increased to 40. " Why did they not count out? " Why, because the Government did not wish it, as they were certain of a majority; and the Opposition knew that it was no use to try " a count," for though only 35 were in the House there were within the sound of bell enough members to make four or five Houses.

It was a good piece of diplomacy after all of Lord Palmerston to allow the debate to go on to the third night, for during the interval the " whip " was so effectually used that there were many more Members present on the third than there had been on the second night. For on the adjourned division only 416 voted, and the Government majority was but 70, but on the next night 503 voted on Mr. Seymer's amendment, and on the main question 479, and the final majority for Ministers was 127. Take this instance to show the exertions which were made : An Hon. Member was down at his seat in North Wales. He received the summons at 2 p.m. on Thursday; he started off immediately, drove seven miles to the rail, arrived at the House at 11.35, and voted for the Government.

Mr. Disraeli rose about 10 o'clock ; there were not more than 250 members to listen; but when it became known throughout the building that he was up the House filled rapidly, and long before he closed was crowded with members. Every part was full. The body of the House, the side-galleries, and the standing room below the bar were all crammed. We have often been asked whether the House will hold all the 654 Members ? Well, we should say, from its appearance on Thursday, that it will not. It appeared to us to be then uncomfortably full ; and yet there were at least 150 Members not there : 500 is an unusually large number. There have been 600 present, but that was at a contested election for a Speaker. After Disraeli came Lord Palmerston.

The indomitable pluck of the Noble Premier was never more shown than on this debate. For a week past he had been racked with the gout, so as to be obliged to clothe one of his feet in a woollen shoe and hobble upstairs with a stick; but still his Lordship was at his post during the whole of the three nights. Other Members, and Cabinet Ministers too, slunk away to eat, and drink, and smoke; but, excepting for a few minutes, the Noble Lord, from "dewy eve to early morn," sat as if fastened to the bench. At 11.30 on Thursday he arose, limped to the table, and, with the weight of his body resting on one limb to save his gouty member, he spoke for an hour as merrily and with as much freedom as he ever did in his life. It is true that there was a good deal in the scene to cheer him and make him for a time "o'er all the ills of life victorious." For a month or two past his position had been doubtful. In several skirmishes he had been worsted. Divisions and strife had prevailed in his camp. But now his old party had concentrated its forces, closed its ranks, and he knew that the pitched battle he was fighting would be crowned with a decisive triumph. Still it must be acknowledged that he is, for physical power and animal spirits, a remarkable man. We question whether there is another man in the Queen's dominions who, at the age of seventy-two and tormented with the gout, could sit seven hours watching a debate and then get up and make a lively and forcible speech of an hour's length.

Mr. Whiteside replied, but of what he said or how he said it we have no knowledge. The House was excessively crowded, the Members impatient; and though they did not attempt to put the Hon. Member down, the buzz of conversation was so great, and the whole scene so distracting, that we could pay no attention to the learned orator. And now the time has come. See, the Speaker is up. All oratory is over. He puts the amendment first—Mr. Ker Seymer's amendment: "That the House postpone the consideration of the fall of Kars until after the discussion on the Treaty of Peace." The form in which the amendment was put was this: Mr. Seymer proposed that all the words after "that" in Mr. Whiteside's motion be left out, and that his (Mr. Seymer's) words be inserted. The Speaker said, "The question which I have to put is—that the words proposed to be left out stand part of the question. All they that are for it, say 'Ay'; they that are against it, say 'No.'" All, therefore, who did not wish to have the amendment shouted "Aye"; and Mr. Seymer's friends "No." In this case the "Ayes" preponderated, and the Speaker declared—"the 'Ayes' have it." He then turned to the mover, Mr. Seymer, and said, "Do you divide?" The Hon. Member took off his hat, in token of assent. "Strangers withdraw," cried the Speaker, and the division proceeded. For Seymer there were 52; against him, 451. After the division was announced the Speaker put the original motion, and another division took place; when there were: for Whiteside, 176; against, 303—majority, 127. Loud and long-continued cheers followed, and a stream of crowding, scuffling, pushing, hurrying, scurrying Members poured out of the House, all anxious to get down stairs to secure cabs and go home. The great fight is over, in five minutes the House has no more than thirty or forty Members in it, and the Clerk is reading "the Orders of the Day."

CHAPTER III.

MR. EDWARD MIALL AND HIS MOTION FOR AN INQUIRY INTO THE REVENUES OF THE STATE CHURCH IN IRELAND AND THEIR DISTRIBUTION.

June 7, 1856. WE have had no attractive debate in the House of late, unless we except the discussion on Mr. Miall's motion for overhauling the revenues of the Irish Church, and that only kept together for a length of time about 150 members. There were more at first, but many went away, and did not come back until the time drew on for the division, when the number rose up to 260, viz., 95 for the resolution, and 165 against. It was expected by some that there would be no House, or if a House should be made, that it would certainly be counted out at dinner time. But Mr. Miall's supporters had managed matters better than was supposed, for at four o'clock the House was unusually full for Tuesday. And even during the dangerous dinner time there were always present over a hundred members. The fact was, that it became known that the supporters of the motion had been very active with the " whip," and so the opponents were obliged to " whip " too, and thus, between the two, all danger of a count-out disappeared.

Mr. Edward Miall, the Hon. Member for Rochdale, is well known throughout a large circle as an earnest and zealous advocate of anti-State Church principles. He was formerly a dissenting minister of Leicester, but in 1841 gave up his charge to establish the *Nonconformist* newspaper, for the express purpose of promoting more extensively his cherished opinions. This was considered at the time, by some of the " stricter sects," a very questionable step, and, moreover, the Dissenters, at least the dissenting ministers, were not prepared for Mr. Miall's advanced views, and so for a long time he had not only to contend against the Church party, who, of course, abused him virulently enough, but also against the half-heartedness, and in not a few cases positive opposition, of those who might naturally have been expected to render him their cordial support. But there were two things which sustained Mr. Miall, and made him conqueror at last, viz., his faith and his great ability. Whether he is right or wrong we do not here discuss, but that he believes in the bottom of his soul that he is right no man can doubt ; nor can any one question that greater ability has never been shown in the advocacy of any cause than that with which Mr. Miall has preached, in the columns of his paper and in his innumerable speeches, the principles which he holds ; and now his paper stands at the head of the dissenting press, and he is a Member of Parliament. And he, whose doctrines were once, and that not long ago, denounced by the Church people as revolutionary, and thought so ultra by dissenters that ministers refused to lend their places of worship for his meetings, and counselled their flocks not to attend, can now expound them to the British Senate, and get 95 members to vote that they are worthy the consideration of the House. Is it not still true, then, that " faith can move mountains " ? We could not help thinking so as we listened to Mr. Miall whilst, for an hour and a half, he expounded and enforced his principles, eliciting the hearty cheers of his friends, and compelling the respectful attention of even his bitterest foes.

Up to the night of this debate Mr. Miall has scarcely been appreciated in the House. He has had much to contend with. In the first place, his antecedents were not such as to secure him favour in the eyes of members of Parliament. " A Radical parson turned politician," " a fellow who has come to upset the Church," was hardly likely to get a hearing from Noble Lords, Gallant Officers, and Country Squires, on the Tory benches. Nor could it be expected that the Whigs would give him much encouragement; for neither do they like " men who come to turn the world upside down." And, further, Mr. Miall's want of physical power will always be a hindrance to him. His voice is thin and weak, and unless the House is predisposed to listen he never can command its attention. All this Mr. Miall is quite conscious of; and therefore it is that he does not often attempt to speak, although his silence sometimes brings down upon him the censure of thoughtless friends outside. But Mr. Miall has succeeded at last, if he never did before; for, by the testimony of friends and foes, it is settled that he not only fully obtained and kept the attention of the House on the occasion of this debate, but delivered a remarkably able and effective speech. We also heard the speech, and fall in with the general opinion. And we can further say that we never saw the House more attentive. The Members were not only quiet, but earnestly listening, that a link in the reasoning might not be dropped, or even a word be lost. And, when the Honourable Member finished, a hearty cheer told him that if he could not carry his motion, he had conquered for himself a new and far higher position in the House of Commons than he had ever attained to before. But really and truly, though the motion was defeated by a majority of seventy, Mr. Miall had achieved a success. In the first place, he had got the House to listen, and, considering the subject and the character of the British Senate, that of itself was no mean achievement. But, when we consider what it was that Mr. Miall proposed to do— nothing less than to lay the axe to the root of the " Protestant Church of Ireland, as by law established "—and that ninety-three, or, inclusive of pairs, about 130, had sanctioned this daring proposition, the result of the debate must be considered an extraordinary circumstance in parliamentary history, and one which foreshadows more extraordinary things in no very distant future.

Much of the success is, no doubt, owing to Mr. Miall's prudent and judicious conduct. For a long time after he became a Member of Parliament there can be no question that he disappointed the expectations of some of his friends. They had heard him speak at public meetings, and had felt his power whilst from the platform he eloquently expounded his views; and they expected that he would carry everything before him in the House, as he had been wont to do in more popular assemblies. But Mr. Miall knew better than even to attempt this; he was well aware that the House of Commons was not a public meeting, and that to speak there effectively on such a subject was altogether a very different matter from writing in the columns of the *Nonconformist* or addressing an assembly of willing listeners at Crosby Hall; and, therefore, notwithstanding the expressed disapprobation of some of his too zealous followers, the sneer of his old dissenting opponents, and the frequent deprecatory remarks which were made in dissenting circles—to wit, " that he had found his level," " that he had promised great things and done nothing," " that he was like all the rest, he had attained his object, got M.P. tacked to his name, and put his principles in his pocket "—he bided his time, never attempted to bully the House, nor obtruded himself and his opinions upon it when it was unwilling to listen. In short, like a wise man, he waited until his turn should come, regardless alike of the sneers of foes and the impatience of friends ; and he has now got his reward.

Feb. 14, 1857. Hitherto we have been very dull. The first night we had some liveliness, but still there was nothing like the excitement which we have seen on such occasions. Mr. Disraeli meant to deliver a great speech, but he certainly failed. The greater part of his harangue was delivered in a confused and bungling manner for a speaker of his reputation. He hesitated, stammered, and at times seemed quite at a loss either for ideas or for language to express them. He spoke early in the evening, when the House was shifting and restless ; and these circumstances don't suit Mr. Disraeli. He seldom speaks well before dinner, and never unless the House is full. Midnight is the time to hear the leader of the Opposition. Mr. Gladstone spoke, of course, well, and so did Lord John Russell. Indeed, it was generally admitted that the Noble Lord delivered the most statesmanlike speech of the evening. Lord Palmerston was, as ever, ingenious, clever, and witty. His retort upon Disraeli was in his happiest vein, and made the House ring with laughter. " The Right Hon. Member," he said, " charges me with cleverly getting my party into difficulties, and cleverly getting it out of them. Well, at all events, I balance the account ; but if the Right Hon. Gentleman had inquired on his own side of the House, he might have heard of a gentleman who, last session, repeatedly got his party into difficulties, and—*could not get it out again.*" It is amusing to watch Lord Palmerston when he is about to bring forth a joke ; you may always

know that something witty is coming. His face suddenly
changes—it seems to get broader and shorter; and as he
approaches to the actual moment of birth, you would hardly
know it as the face of the Noble Lord. And doesn't he
enjoy the joke! When Disraeli makes the House laugh, he
never condescends to laugh himself—a sardonic smile is all
that he indulges in; but Palmerston laughs outright, and
evidently has some difficulty in pulling down his face to due
statesmanlike gravity when he resumes his discourse. He
certainly is a most marvellously tough man; time, and gout,
and labour seem to have no effect upon him.

CHAPTER IV.

THE CANTON DEBATE—THE DIVISION—THE DEFEAT—THE GENERAL ELECTION AND THE RETALIATION — THE SPEAKER'S RETIREMENT.

[The Canton Debate was one of the most important that had come up for years in the House of Commons. The Chinese authorities at Canton had boarded the *Arrow*, a small vessel which professed to be British, but really was not so, and had carried off from her twelve of her crew on a charge of piracy. The *Arrow* was not, in fact, a British vessel, but only a Chinese vessel which had obtained by fraud the temporary possession of an English flag. Our Plenipotentiary at Hong-Kong, Sir John Bowring, acted in a most high-handed fashion, and demanded the surrender of all the men, an apology from the Chinese Government, and a further assurance that nothing of the kind would ever be done again. The Chinese authorities refused, and Canton was thereupon bombarded by the English fleet. Mr. Cobden brought forward a motion in the House of Commons declaring " that the papers which have been laid upon the table fail to establish satisfactory grounds for the violent measures resorted to at Canton in the late affair of the *Arrow*." He was supported by Gladstone, Disraeli, Lord John Russell, Lord Robert Cecil (now Lord Salisbury), Mr. Roebuck, Sir E. Bulwer-Lytton,

afterwards the first Lord Lytton, and a number of other
leading men of all parties.]

March 7, 1857. THE great and all-absorbing parliamentary
topic of the week has been the Canton debate.
The excitement in the House and the Lobby has been
intense—unequalled by anything of the sort that has occurred
since the great Corn-Law contest. The Lobby has been so
crowded, that it has been only with the greatest exertion
that the police could keep a clear passage to the House for
the Members ; and all the galleries, from four o'clock until
the House broke up, have been on every night of the debate
filled ; and there have been besides hundreds of eager and
anxious expectants waiting about the House for admittance ;
and then, many of them—indeed most of them—did wait
all the night, and went home disappointed at last. Members' orders they could get, and seemed astonished that,
though they had this talismanic paper, they could not get
in, forgetting that though, when there is room, this slip of
paper is a veritable "open-sesame," yet there is one thing
that it cannot do—it cannot make space. An order is a good
thing to have when there is room, but when there is not it
is as useless as a cheque upon a bank at which there are
"no effects."   Poor fellows ! we could not help pitying
them as we saw them jammed together, knowing, as we
did, the utter hopelessness of their case. Many of them
had come up from the country on purpose to hear the
debate, relying upon the omnipotence of their Members,
and some, perhaps, had never been in the House in their
lives. "What, cannot you get me in?" we heard one say to
his Member. "Oh, do try! I never heard a debate, and
I have come to town on purpose to hear this." "My dear
fellow, what am I to do?" was the answer, "every place
is full." "Can't you ask the Speaker to put me *some-*

where?" "Impossible; the Speaker himself couldn't put his own brother in where there is no room."

Nor was the excitement amongst the members less marked, and, *crescit eundo*, it increased as the debate went on. It is true that in the early part of the first evening the members did not seem to be awake to the importance of the crisis. That there was to be a stout fight, everybody knew; but it was generally considered that a majority for Government was secure. But when Mr. Cobden had delivered his masterly speech, and in his quiet but telling way had unrolled before the House his terrible indictment, and when it was made known by the cheering which came from all parts of the House what numbers of Members, of all parties, were prepared to support the Hon. Member for the West Riding, then a change came over the spirit of the House, and especially over the Government side. It became apparent that this contest was no child's play, and that if the Government meant to resist successfully this formidable attack, they not only had not a moment to lose, but that every art and manœuvre which the science and skill of the "Whips" could bring to bear must be put in requisition. Everybody accustomed to political contests in the House was aware of this change. It might be seen in the looks of the Ministers on the Treasury Bench; Hayter's face betrayed it—all calm and imperturbable as it generally is; and the knots of members about the lobbies and in the waiting-rooms—some quietly, and some violently discussing the subject—showed that a crisis of no ordinary importance was at hand.

But the excitement was at its height when Lord John Russell delivered his remarkable speech. During the whole of the evening there had been anxious questionings about the way in which Lord John would vote, and but few seemed to be quite decided upon the point until he arose in the House. His Lordship did not, however, leave the House long in doubt; he very soon showed that he not only meant to support Mr. Cobden, but that he intended also to carry all his followers with him; and when he sat down, after having delivered one of the most telling speeches that we have heard for some years past, things looked very gloomy indeed for the Ministry, and many an Under-Secretary and junior Lord began to shake in his shoes. Indeed, there can be no doubt that if the division had come off on that night Government would have been defeated by a large majority. But that was not to be—trust Palmerston and Hayter for that! Nor was it to be on Friday, the next night. Before Friday night many a message had been despatched by post and by telegraph, and the large increase in the number of members on Friday showed that all this had not been done without effect. But still further time was required to make things at all pleasant, and the long interval between Friday and Monday night would be invaluable to the Government. In the first place, it would give still further time for members to come up from a distance, and then, secondly (and this is even more important), it would afford opportunity for the appliance of those mysterious arts and powerful incantations at which your Ministerial " Whips " are such adepts. Exactly what these Circean arts are no one knows but the initiated, but that they are of wondrous power is certain and not to be disputed. Many a fond dream of independence have they dissipated, and many an indignant patriotic feeling have they damped down, but how it is done must ever remain a mystery to all but those who are behind the scenes. And so on Friday the debate was again adjourned.

On Monday—and the change was apparent—the Government had recovered from its panic—and the troublous nervousness observable in Hayter's face had passed away

—letters had been received, books examined, and it had become apparent that things were not so bad as they seemed —Mr. Hayter was himself again, and the Lords of the Treasury and the Admiralty began to see prospects of salaries beyond the coming quarter-day.

The most extraordinary speech during the debate was unquestionably Mr. Whiteside's. We have heard the learned gentleman deliver many wonderful harangues, but this was the most wonderful of all. We don't mean as to matter, but manner. The matter was reported duly in the morning papers; but who can describe the manner? As we witnessed the gesticulations, how we longed for Cruikshank or Leech to be there, that the orator might be presented in one, even if only one, of his wonderful positions; but, alas! no artist is allowed in the House, and words are altogether powerless. We remember Edward Irving, and we have seen many an actor "tearing a passion to tatters," but nothing comes up to Whiteside.

Since the above was written the smash has come. In a House of 510 Members, at half-past two o'clock on the morning of Wednesday, the Government was beaten by a majority of sixteen. Up to the last the event was uncertain; such was the confusion of parties, that no one could calculate accurately who would win. As the moment for dividing came the excitement throughout the House grew more intense than ever, and so crowded were the Peers' Seats and Diplomatic Galleries, that it was with the utmost difficulty they were cleared in time. In fact, the Diplomatic Gallery was not cleared, for one unfortunate foreigner was shut in, and very perplexed he looked when he was made to understand that he was in custody, and not less so when, after due consultation held with the Speaker, the Sergeant opened the door and drove him to the outer Lobby. The Duke of Cambridge and members of the diplomatic corps, the Russian, American, Austrian Ministers, &c., not only sat patiently listening to the debate, but waited outside until the numbers were declared. The great speech of the debate was Gladstone's. Some went so far as to say that it was the greatest harangue that he ever delivered. The cheers whilst he spoke were almost incessant. Palmerston's speech evidently produced but little effect. Poor old man! it was painful to see him hobbling upstairs on two sticks to fight such a battle. It is bad enough at seventy-four years of age to sit from five o'clock till one, and then to rise and reply in a speech of an hour to such opponents as Gladstone and Cobden, Russell and Graham, but to have to contend with the gout as well must be anything but pleasant. Well, we suppose that the Palmerston Ministry is at an end, unless the plucky Premier should dissolve. And now, Mr. Cobden, "What next? and next?"

Mar. 14, 1857. In three weeks from this time, or thereabouts, the Right Hon. Charles Shaw Lefevre, who has for eighteen years occupied the Chair of the House of Commons as its Speaker, will vanish from the scene which he has so long adorned, and "the place which knows him now will know him no more for ever." For a long time past rumours have been afloat that this would be his last Parliament, but it was not until last Monday that he formally announced that he really intended to retire. As soon as this announcement had been made, Lord Palmerston gave notice that on the following day he should move a vote of thanks to the Right Hon. Gentleman, and also an address to the Crown, praying that a suitable acknowledgment may be made for his long and faithful services. It was no wonder, then, that on Tuesday afternoon, at half-past four, the House was unusually full ; for what Member of the House who could possibly get down would fail to be present to show his respect to so old and faithful a servant?

May 9, 1857.
" My Noble Lords and Gentlemen,
Once more we're met together again,
When last we met I said so then."—*Punch*.

To one unaccustomed to parliamentary life the scene on Thursday, the 30th of April, when the new Parliament assembled after the general election, was strange and ludicrous. It was one o'clock when we arrived at the House, and though it wanted a full hour to the time fixed for the assembling of the Members, it was evident to us that a number of the " new 'uns," as the policemen call those who have not been in Parliament before, were already loitering about the palace. It was clear that they were not "strangers," as they had been, after due questioning, suffered to go into parts of the building where no strangers are allowed to go, and it was also equally certain they were not old Members. They had not yet got the parliamentary air and bearing, and, moreover, were evidently puzzled to find their way about, rushing into all manner of out-of-the-way places into which they did not want to go, and altogether unable to discover the places to which they did want to go. One old man we found peeping into a washing-room, and on politely inquiring whether we could be of any service we discovered that he was hunting for the library, which was some hundred yards off. Another seemed to us to be regularly surveying the building, for there was not a door that he did not open on his way, nor a recess that he did not look into, but as he was wholly unacquainted with the plan of the " Mighty Maze," twice he came round to the spot whence he started ; and, when we ceased watching him, he was just blundering into the private room of one of the officers of the House. At half-past one there were some thirty or forty " new 'uns " in the House, and from a quarter before two to the time fixed they came up in such a stream that the doorkeepers must have been perfectly bewildered. At ten minutes past two the scene in the House, from the reporters' gallery, was very odd to those who are old attendants upon the House. The few old Members who were present, and some of the new who had personal friends to show them where to go, quietly took their seats, but the bulk of the " new 'uns " stood hustling about the bar, and all with their hats on, to the great discomfort and disgust of the sergeant and deputy-sergeant, who were both on duty, vainly striving to reduce the chaos to something like order. Amongst the old Members Sir James Graham was conspicuous, stalwart and fresh as ever—but how changed was all around him since he last sat there! Cobden, Bright, Gibson, Cardwell, Phillimore, Layard, Fox, and Miall, who sat in that neigh-bourhood, are all gone. The Right Hon. Baronet did not seem, however, to be much affected by his bereavement, for we never saw him look better, and he appeared to enjoy the contemplation of the surging crowd below him amazingly. Soon afterwards Sidney Herbert came in and Gladstone, but they could not take their wonted seats, as they had long been occupied by "nobody knows who." Palmerston was in his usual place, but his Lordship is not much the better for the relaxation of the recess. He has lost all his springiness, still wears shoes made more for ease than show, looks pale, and shows unmistakable signs of a disposition to stoop. " Ah! it's no use," said an Honourable Member, shaking his head, " if the Opposition can't beat him old age and the gout will." Lord John Russell was there ; but, as his place was occupied, he dropped down at the extreme end of the Treasury bench. The

Noble Lord is quite up to the mark. We should guess that he has been breathing the country air since his election; for, instead of that chalky paleness which is almost invariably the mark of an old Member of Parliament, he has the bronzed look of a country gentleman fresh from his estate. Mr. Robert Lowe looked, as he sat on the step of the gangway, fresh as he always has looked since the hour of his birth, and as he will look until the day of his death. His is a face that nothing can change. Sir Charles Wood was also present; still the same jaunty gentleman, with hat stuck aside and hands in his breeches' pockets; always the same, "whether he win or lose the game." On the Opposition benches there were very few old Members. Walpole was there in his usual place, but Disraeli was not—he mistook the hour of meeting; nor was Henley, Whiteside, Pakington, or Bulwer-Lytton present. Amongst the "new 'uns" known to us, conspicuous above all was the burly, corpulent Sir John Potter, Mr. Bright's substitute, unquestionably the "greatest man" in the House. We should lay him at eighteen stone, and should not be surprised to hear that twenty will not "fetch him up." He looked about for a long while for Mr. Kinglake, and at last discovered him amongst the crowd. But we will say nothing of him here; the author of "Eothen" must have a special notice. The grey head of the veteran political warrior, General Thompson, the man who opened fire against the Corn Laws before many of the League were born, was easily discovered. The old General must be far on the shady side of seventy, and yet how active he is! Query—Is it wise of him, unless he wishes to die on his shield, to come again into the stormy arena of politics? We know not whether any more "gods" were among the crowd; but if there were they must be " *Dii minores*," unknown to us.

CHAPTER V.

Aug. 15, 1857. LET us take our stand in the outer lobby, and for a short time notice the parliamentary and other notables, great and small, as they pass by. We can see them better here than in the House. It requires a practised eye to know members in the House, especially when they have their hats on, as the light descending from the ceiling throws the face into shade. We have known honourable members look half an hour for a friend in the House without success, although the said friend has been there all the while; but in the lobby there is no such difficulty. Who is that tall, manly fellow with collar turned down and a strong walking-stick in his hand? That is the Honourable Charles Sumner, the member of the American Senate who was assaulted by Brooks. He is a constant attendant here. Through the favour of the Speaker he has the *entrée* when he chooses. To-night the debate on the Divorce Bill is to come on and he hopes to hear Gladstone speak. He is a very fine-looking man, and has the reputation of being an orator himself. He has a large circle of acquaintance in London amongst the men of the Shaftesbury school. He was introduced to the Speaker by Lord Ebrington. The

Bishop, who is striding across the lobby, is Samuel Wilber-
force, of Oxford. It is the Divorce debate that has attracted
him. He is not an infrequent attendant upon the House.
You see he also marches in without question by the doorkeeper. All bishops who are peers of Parliament have a
right to go in. Other bishops have to seek permission like
common folk. You see there are no signs of fasting and
maceration about the right reverend father, albeit he is a
member of the school which patronises such things. On
the contrary, he is inclined to be corpulent in person, has
a jolly, good-humoured face, and, as we can testify, is fond
of launching a joke, and can laugh heartily at the jokes
of others. But here comes my Lord Derby : the gentleman
there in spectacles. You are disappointed by his appearance?
Well, most people are at first sight. We were ourselves.
Our imagination had painted the representative of the house
of Stanley as a tall, stalwart, broad-shouldered baron ; but
you see he is nothing of the sort. The fact is that but few
of the members of our oldest families are large men. There
are about a dozen men in the House of Commons of the
height of six feet, but with one or two exceptions they are
all of plebeian origin. The Stanleys, the Gordons, the
Russells, the Duffs, the Lennoxes, &c., are none of them
above the average, and some of them below it.

But let us call your attention to the old gentleman who is
coming from the library, for he is a special favourite of ours,
and, indeed, of all those who know him. We mean the
short, white-headed old man without his hat—that is Major-
General Perronet Thompson, member for Bradford. "And
who is General Thompson ?" Ah! it is a sign you are
but a youth, or you could not have failed to hear of
General Thompson ; for perhaps, on the whole, there is no
more remarkable man in the House of Commons. First, he
may be said to be the Father of Free Trade—for when

Bright was only a boy of fifteen, and Cobden a youth of twenty-one, General Thompson had worked out the theory, and settled it upon so firm a basis in his famous "Catechism of the Corn Laws," that from that time the principle was settled—and all that had to be done was to agitate for its adoption. All due honour to Cobden and Bright and the rest of the League; but, after all, they were only the workers—the thinker was unquestionably Thomas Perronet Thompson. "Did you ever read the 'Catechism of the Corn Laws?'" said an eminent member of the League to us some twenty years ago. "No." "Then read it, for there you will find all the arguments that our agitators have ever used, and many more that they could not use, because they did not understand them." Nor is this the only thing that the good old General has done. He was first a midshipman—then became a soldier—was once Governor of Sierra Leone, and it is said that he is the only governor who came home uninjured in health—and further, he was for a time in the thick of the Napoleonic wars—has been to India —is a great mathematician—profound musical theorist—has written innumerable articles, pamphlets, &c.; and as to languages, can talk in most of the tongues of the babbling earth. Not a foreigner comes to the lobby but may have a chat with the old General—turbaned Turk, strangely tiled Parsee, Hindu Rajah, or swallow-tailed European—it is all the same to General Thompson. The Honourable and Gallant Gentleman does not often speak now, but when he does he generally utters something that cleaves into the very heart of the question. Take, for instance, his saying about the Chinese poisonings—"Three hundred poisoned and not one dead? Why, I will defy all the physicians in Europe to poison three hundred people, *and not kill one.*" The old gentleman shakes his head over this Indian mutiny. "Ah," said he to a friend of ours, "there must have been something wrong going on; for those sepoys, if they had been kindly treated, would much rather have nursed the babies than shot the fathers and mothers." And then he went on to tell the following story as an illustration of the danger of interfering with the religious feelings of the natives :—" When I was in India, I was going one day to my tent, and seeing a circle of earth with a fire in the middle, I jumped over it; and what was my surprise to receive soon after a deputation of sepoys to inform me that by so doing I had so polluted their dinner which was cooking that the whole of it had been thrown away. 'Well,' said I, ' what am I to do?' 'Oh!' said the speaker, ' the sahib must give us money to buy us another dinner,' which request of course I immediately complied with." The old General is now seventy-four years, but Time has laid his hand lightly upon him. He can attend the house from four till three in the morning, and then walk home. We saw him creeping along Parliament Street last week, in the broad daylight, when the hands of the Horse Guards clock were pointing to 3.45 a.m.

The old gentleman whom you see walking with slow and stately pace across the lobby is Sir Richard Bethell, M.P. for Aylesbury, and her Majesty's Attorney-General. He has a stern battle to fight to-night, for he has to take the lead in working his Divorce Bill through Committee against a host of powerful and bitter foes. And, further, he will have to fight almost alone. Sir George Grey may occasionally come to his help, and Lord Palmerston may now and then throw in a shot, but as it is a " legal measure," the principal burthen must fall upon our Attorney-General. Sir Henry Keating, the Solicitor-General, ought to be a good auxiliary; but he is new to his office, and, between ourselves, does not seem to be a very efficient addition to the debating power of the Government. But Mr. Attorney, though opposed by all

the talent of the Opposition, having Henley, Lord John
Manners, Disraeli, Malins, &c., on his front, and Mr. Gladstone on his right flank, will be found quite a match for
them all; for on such questions as this there is not a man
in the House comparable in debate to Sir Richard
Bethell. When you first hear him speak you will probably be disappointed, for there is a good deal of affecta-
tion in his manner, and he has a lisp in his utterance which,
if you were to shut your eyes, would make you think you
were listening to an affected young lady; but give him your
attention, and you will soon find that you have no ordinary
man before you. His knowledge is amazing, his dexterity
in unravelling a legal entanglement is unrivalled. Nor is he
wanting in quickness of retort, as you will soon perceive.
And as to his style, though he makes no pretensions to the
flowing oratory of Gladstone, yet in " choosing the right
word for the right place" he is Gladstone's superior. Indeed
it may be said of the Hon. Member for the University of
Oxford and Sir Richard, as was said by Fox of Pitt and
himself : Gladstone never wants *a* word, but Bethell never
wants *the* word. Of course, Gladstone is far away the greater
orator of the two ; but give Bethell his subject, and in a
close, sharp fight in Committee he is at all times the great
orator's match. You see the Learned Gentleman has under
his arm a bundle of briefs. He always walks into the House
thus loaded, that he may employ the intervals between the
debates in which he is not wanted in preparing, in some
snug recess in the division-lobby, for his Chancery duties.
The Learned Gentleman is said to be one of the hardest
workers in the House ; and it is clear that he cannot be an
idler, or he never could keep abreast of the heavy duties
which, while Parliament is sitting, are laid upon him.
Sixteen hours a day for labour, and eight for meals and
sleep, we imagine is something like the division of his time.

Recreation, as it is called, he cannot dream of until the vacation comes; and yet, like all really hard workers, Sir Richard never seems to be in a hurry.

Feb. 13, 1858. Mr. Roebuck has come out in fine feather this session. For several years past he has looked like a moulting bird, and when he attempted to speak he painfully reminded us of a sickly game-cock trying to crow. Two years ago it will be remembered that, on his moving for a committee on Crimean matters, he could not go on with his speech, but after about ten minutes' trial he sank into his seat exhausted with the effort; and the Honourable Member, who had before been long ailing, had not recovered his pristine vigour until this session. His voice last session, though improved, was still feeble, and his whole bearing and manner were very different from those of the Roebuck of former years. But now Roebuck " is himself again." Of course he looks older than he did before his illness. His hair is thinned and grey, his features are sharper, and his shoulders are rounder; but all this may be traced to age, for he is fifty-seven. The sickness under which the Honourable Member so long languished appears to be entirely gone. He walks now without support; his voice rings through the House as it used to do when he was the pet Radical member for Bath ; and his action is just as dramatic as it was a dozen years ago. We are sincerely glad to see the renewal of his strength ; for whatever opinion we may hold of the Honourable Member's prudence at times, we should sorely feel John Arthur Roebuck's absence from the House. Amongst the circumlocutionist trash which is now the fashion of the House, it is refreshing occasionally to listen to the direct, manly, vigorous denunciations of the olden time. He hits hard—no doubt often harder than is necessary—and his asperity of language, intensified into an appearance of malignity by the tones of his voice, his scornful looks, and his emphatic action, we could sometimes wish to be a little softened down ; but he tells plain truths which need to be told, and is the able organ in the House of feelings and opinions held by a large portion of the community which ought to have utterance. The conduct of Louis Napoleon in giving sanction to the addresses of the gasconading colonels by publishing them in the *Moniteur* was a fine theme for Mr. Roebuck, and it was capital fun to hear him in his "unadorned," but biting, eloquence denounce the quondam refugee, and to see the dismay on the faces of Ministers as he remorselessly trampled down all the delicate precautions which Lord Palmerston and his colleagues had carefully spun to make everything "pleasant and agreeable to all parties." His reply to Mr. Bowyer, "the Pope's advocate " in the House, was capital. Mr. Roebuck was telling the House how Louis Napoleon had restored the pension which had been awarded by the Great Napoleon to the man who attempted to assassinate the Duke of Wellington, when he was interrupted by an emphatic cry of "No, no." "Yes, yes," replied Mr. Roebuck. "No, no," the voice repeated ; when, turning round, and seeing that the voice was Mr. Bowyer's, Mr. Roebuck looked at him for a moment, and then, in his bitterest manner, said: "The Honourable Member is an advocate of the King of Naples. I won't answer *him*." The House was uproarious with delight at this terrible "facer," and it was a long time before it resumed its quietude.

Mr. Bright took his seat on Tuesday night, greeted, as he marched up to the table between Mr. J. B. Smith and Mr. Louis Ricardo, by the loud cheers of the House. The Hon. Member looked healthy, though he is not nearly so bulky as he was. When he retired from the table he was heartily shaken by the hand by all sorts of members. Even the solemn Mr. Newdegate congratulated his old opponent on his reappearance.

Feb. 27, 1858. Thursday night was the last of the debate on the first reading of the India Bill, and the most important, for the great guns opened fire, and the division took place, which gave the Government the large majority of 145. Colonel Sykes led off the evening with a long business-like speech in favour of the Company, which if it did not win votes was listened to with profound attention by a crowded House, and gained the speaker great credit. It was the first real defence of the Company which had been offered. It took nearly three hours to deliver, and must have employed the Gallant Colonel as many days to get up. Colonel Sykes is an "Old Indian." He joined the Bombay army in 1804, and did not finally leave India until 1831. He has been a Director many years, and has also been Chairman and Vice-Chairman of the Company. He had therefore a claim to be heard. Mr. Willoughby, another Director, followed on the same side, and Sir Charles Wood and Lord John Russell *per contra;* but the most attractive speech was one delivered by our famous novelist, Sir Edward George Earle Lytton Bulwer-Lytton. We all know when the Honourable Baronet means to speak. He enters the House early in the evening, to reconnoitre—wanders out again—meanders through the lobbies, down the corridors into the library, &c., evidently ruminating and studying his speech, and when the time approaches generally settles down on the front bench on the Opposition side, near Mr. Disraeli. Sir Bulwer-Lytton's speeches as compositions are not excelled by anything that the House listens to. The topics are well chosen; the matter is admirably arranged; the style is thoroughly English, and the composition is faultless; but the whole is marred and rendered ineffective by the strange voice in which it is uttered, and the extravagant action by which it is accompanied. The voice of the Honourable Baronet is not naturally unmusical, but it is spoiled by a singularly inartistic modulation, and by a habit of clanging out certain words *ore rotundo*, as if the speaker meant to imitate the blast of a trumpet, by which they are broken up into echoes, and as intelligible words are entirely lost to the listeners. If you sit near the Honourable Baronet, apply your hand to your ear to concentrate the sounds, and listen attentively, you may possibly catch every word in his sentences, but not otherwise. Of course this defect is a fatal drawback to the effect of his speeches. Let us give an instance. On Thursday night the Baronet had been arguing that the councillors would not be free from the control of the president and the Government, and, in short, they would be little more than clerks. "Now," said the speaker, "if they are to be clerks, call them so; but if they are to be councillors, they must be free." A very good climax this, and one which, if it had been well delivered, would have told well upon the House; but unfortunately the word "free," which is the key to the whole sentence, was lost. It was a mere noise—might have been "fra," or "bah," or "yah;" but what it really was meant to be no one could guess, excepting those who sat very near. Those who did catch it cheered, and then others cheered also; but for some time afterwards we could see and hear that the bulk of the Members had lost the key-word of the passage, and when the Honourable Baronet was progressing with his speech, instead of listening they were anxiously asking "what was the word?" And if the voice of the Honourable Baronet is strange, his action is equally so. It is not quite so extravagant as Mr. Whiteside's, for there is a method discernible in Sir Bulwer-Lytton's gesticulation, but Mr. Whiteside's movements partake largely of the character of St. Vitus's dance. Still Sir Bulwer-Lytton's are extravagant enough, and quite beyond all our powers of description without a series of diagrams to help us. And now, before we part with Sir Bulwer-Lytton, we must say a word or two upon his personal appearance. Reader, did you ever see the worthy Baronet? If not, you have yet an extraordinary sight to see, for Sir Bulwer-Lytton's face is a wonder. It is not naturally deformed, or even ugly, or we would not comment upon it, for we have never dwelt in these articles on natural personal defects. Sir Bulwer-Lytton's face, it is true, is a marvel, but it is a marvel of his own making; and all that is strange about it might be removed in half an hour by a village barber. It is simply a case of bad cultivation. A comb, a pair of scissors, and a razor would, in skilful hands, metamorphose him into a personable man, which at present he certainly is not. He has a capital forehead, a prominent, but not a bad nose, and we suspect that he has good features generally, but we cannot vouch for this, for they are for the most part entirely concealed by an extraordinary growth of hair. Indeed Sir Bulwer-Lytton seems to be a Nazarite, for certainly no scissors or razor, nor, as we imagine, even a comb, is ever allowed to come near his head. His hair proper is all dishevelled and unkempt, and his beard and moustache grow according to their own will. We have many extraordinary beards and moustaches in the House : we have flowing beards, and stubby beards, and curly beards ; we have moustaches light and delicate like a lady's eyebrow, long and pendant like a Chinaman's, bushy and fierce like a brigand's. Some men wear beard, whiskers, and moustaches ; others shave the whiskers and beard and leave the moustache ; whilst others preserve the moustache and part of the beard, but eschew whiskers ; but in all these varieties, and a great many more, there are marks of design. But Sir Bulwer-Lytton despises all art, and lets Nature take her own way, and the result is probably the most astonishing human face in the world.

CHAPTER VI.

THE "CONSPIRACY TO MURDER" BILL—NEMESIS.

[The Bill to increase the punishment for conspiracy to murder was brought in by Lord Palmerston in 1858. It was a consequence of Orsini's attempt on the life of the Emperor of the French. The Imperial Government, in an almost vehement despatch, called upon England to make her laws more severe against conspiracy to murder. Lord Palmerston brought in the Bill, which was condemned by public opinion as a truckling to the demand of Louis Napoleon. The Bill was rejected in the House of Commons on the motion for its second reading by a majority of 19, and Palmerston and his colleagues resigned office.]

Feb. 27, 1858. THE week ending the 20th of February was eventful. At the beginning the Government seemed "firm as Ailsa Rock"; at the end it was in ruins. Up to Friday night its majorities on all occasions this session had been overwhelming. The Church-rate division, on the preceding Wednesday, which at first sight seems to be an exception, was not really one, for the Church-rate matter has for several years been an "open question" with the Government, many Members of the Government always voting on the popular side. But on Friday night the division on the "Conspiracy to Murder Bill" was a "floorer," and it was seen at once that the Government, after such a defeat, must resign. We do not believe that before the middle of the evening on Friday there was any widely extended suspicion that the Ministry would be in a minority. It was about eight o'clock that the possibility loomed upon us. It was clear then there was fear on the side of the Government, and it was equally clear that hope was animating and swelling the hearts of the Opposition; for Mr. Hayter and Mr. Brand on the Government side, and Colonel Taylor and Mr. Whitmore for the Conservatives, were at work like slaves. And there were evident signs also of the coming event in the hilarity of the Opposition "whips," and the silence and anxious looks of their opponents. Mr. Hayter's face seldom betrays his feelings, but he certainly looked uncomfortable that night. And yet, recollecting that remarkable majority on the first reading, a defeat seemed to be impossible. How could a majority of 200 be turned into a minority? But it was done. And we will now in a few words describe how it came to pass. First, then, let it be remembered that a division on the introduction of a measure is not an accurate criterion of the feeling of the House, because it is considered by many only courteous to allow, as a matter of course, the introduction of a measure, and especially is it considered so with respect to Government Bills. It is argued thus: "This measure is not yet before us. We have only had the outline of it; let it be introduced and printed in regular form, and then we shall see what it really is, and be able to arrive at a correct judgment upon it." To throw out a Government measure on the first reading, or rather to refuse to allow it to be introduced, is an exceptional case. It will be seen, therefore, that the members who voted for the first reading of the Bill were not committed to its approval. Still there can be no doubt that on the first reading the great majority of the supporters of the measure on this occasion meant to vote for it in all its stages ; and we have reason to know that the Government thought it quite safe; and so it would have been safe, but for one influence which was brought to bear upon the members, the strength of which the Government had not accurately gauged. They did not dream of the stir that this measure would make in the country. The House received the Bill favourably, and, at the time, meant to pass it ; but before the second reading came on there arose from below such an ominous growl that members grew alarmed for their seats. One Honourable Member told us that he had received a letter from his political agent warning him not to give any further support to the measure, for that at least four-fifths of his constituents were furiously against it. Another said that " his people " had sent him a very decided requisition. In short, there can be no doubt that it was " the people that did it."

Our readers have of course noticed the remarkable fact that Lord Palmerston, who, not a year ago, was rejoicing when Parliament assembled that the men who had led on the attack upon his Chinese policy were all out, is now dethroned by those very men. That phalanx on the flank of the Government below the gangway is becoming a very formidable body, and, whether for good or evil, will make itself heard and its power felt more than it has done. Lord Palmerston affected contempt for it, which was not wise.

Great was the excitement, in and out of the House, to learn how the division would go ; and when the burst of cheering inside announced to the outsiders that the Ministry were defeated, everybody rushed down and away to spread the intelligence abroad. The Foreign Ambassadors, who were anxiously waiting in the lobby for the news, seemed to be stunned, and could hardly realise the great fact. Lord

Palmerston's closing speech, it is said, showed that the Noble Lord's temper failed him; but we did not notice this. He spoke forcibly—and perhaps something more than forcibly; but we saw no indication of temper. But that he was not received with that respect which has always been paid to him cannot be doubted. It was, perhaps, the first time that the Noble Lord's remarks were received with derisional "Oh, oh's"—may it be the last; for whatever may have been his mistakes, this venerable statesman deserves better than that from an English House of Commons.

The crowd in the lobby was greater on Monday night than we ever saw it before. It was a compact mass of men. And the capacity of Sir Charles Barry's chamber was severely tried, and found wanting. It would not hold the Members; and the peers' seats and the ambassadors' galleries were overflowing, and numbers had to stand in the passages. And yet there was nothing to hear. When the business of the evening really came on, it was all over in two minutes. It consisted in little more than a motion of adjournment until Friday. The House will then meet, and if meanwhile the Ministry be formed, the writs will be moved, and the House adjourned again.

March 6, 1858. For six years the Liberal party in the House of Commons have occupied the seats on the right of the Speaker without interruption; but on Friday evening we saw another sight—a sight to which we are so unaccustomed that the House appeared to our practised eye a scene of strange confusion and disorder. In the main every man in the House has a place, but now every one was out of place, and it will be a long time before we shall feel accustomed to this sudden and unexpected change. Indeed we very much question whether we shall be allowed time enough to get used to it, for it is next to impossible that the

Conservatives can hold for any length of time their position with that formidable Opposition in the van. On entering the House we found a goodly number of the Opposition in their places, while only a small body of the Government party had settled down in theirs. Many of the Members were wandering about the body of the House undecided where they should alight. These, for the most part, were independent members who voted against the Government in the late decisive division, and had helped to throw the Ministry out. Were they now to settle themselves among the supporters of the party which they had so lately helped to defeat?—that seemed an anomalous course. Or were they to join themselves with the Conservatives, to whom, on most subjects, they are entirely opposed? However, in a short time these floating atoms all settled down, and the two parties concreted by natural gravitation and attraction, much as they were before, with the exception that the Liberals and Tories changed sides.

There were, however, a few of the Liberals, or those who have ranked as such, who refused to budge. For instance, Sir James Graham, as soon as the house opened, planted himself resolutely, and without hesitation, in his old place; soon afterwards Roebuck and Drummond also took their accustomed seats. Then Gladstone came in, and every eye watched him to see where he would settle, but his movements showed no hesitation; he had evidently made up his mind, for he went straight to his old seat by the side of Sir James. The next man of note that came in was Lord Palmerston, but his course was straight and unwavering. For six years, and indeed, with very few and very short intervals, ever since the year 1809, the Noble Lord has sat on the right of the Speaker; but on that night he walked with his usual rapid and firm step into the left division-lobby, came into the House at the back of the Speaker's chair, and sat down exactly opposite his old post—as nearly as possible in the very seat from which Disraeli used for so long a time, and until very recently, to hurl his sarcasms and philippics against the " Noble Lord opposite." As soon as Lord Palmerston was seen his adherents cheered vociferously. The rest of the late Ministers, as they came in, joined their old chief. Mr. Hayter made his appearance, but did not stop. He just looked round, and then, without a word or smile for any one, buttoned up his coat, went straight out of the House, and vanished. For the present his occupation is gone. Report says that he was found wanting in the Premier's hour of need, and that if he had used his accustomed energy in "whipping" the catastrophe might have been averted. The *Saturday Review*, on the contrary, hints that the defeat was courted by Lord Palmerston, and that Hayter had received his orders not to " whip " very earnestly. It is said that a more ignominious defeat on the "great Clanricarde question " was certain, and that Lord Palmerston preferred dying in a nobler struggle. But all this we do not give credence to for a moment. Mr. Hayter did " whip "; but, to his great dismay, many of the members would not answer, and many of those that did " went against us." Well might the Right Honourable Gentleman (Baronet, it is said, now) gloomily fly from the House on Friday night. He had nothing to do there. But let no one suppose that Hayter's occupation is utterly gone. Wait a fortnight and you shall see him in the lobby, busy as ever; and, unless the auguries deceive us, he will be there as " Government Whip " before many months have passed over his head.

Lord John Russell—or, as he is familiarly and almost universally called in the House, " Johnny "—came in rather late, and for a time he stood below the bar, with glass at eye, evidently reconnoitring as from a height the position of the forces. Being small of stature, he was not observed by the House generally, but those who were near him showed manifest signs of interest in his movements. And "where will he go?" though you did not hear it, was evidently the question which Members were whispering into their neighbours' ears. For a time he seemed to be undecided. Should he take the corresponding position to that which he lately occupied—" three pair back?" That would be undignified; or should he perch upon the front bench of the Opposition, amongst those whom he had so lately helped to fork out of office? That would scarcely be good taste. To place himself amongst the Tories was of course out of the question. Lord John amongst the Tories! Why, it would almost justify a special sermon from Dr. Cumming, to prove that the last days are really come. After a few minutes the point was settled, and Lord John took his seat in the front ranks of the Opposition, but below the gangway.

Of course the Conservative leaders were not there : they are all out of Parliament. Having accepted office, they *ipso facto* had vacated their seats. But all the subalterns who were present were in high glee—they could not disguise their exultation. To be once more on the sunny side of the House—once more to handle the despatch-boxes, and to be everywhere recognised as belonging to the Government—seemed to have imparted new life to them ; but we apprehend they must have had some twinges of misgiving when they went into the House and saw that compact and formidable body of foes which crowded the Opposition benches, and then looked at their friends on the other side ; for we never saw the Liberals in greater force, excepting on some "great night." Every bench was crowded ; the steps of the gangway were occupied by squatters ; a crowd clustered behind the Speaker's chair, and not a few were obliged to mount into the gallery above, while on the

Government side there was ample room for all, and gaps of unoccupied seats to spare. We know not how the few gentlemen on the Treasury benches felt as they faced this array, and looked back at their own thin ranks; but we could see no other prospect before them than a speedy return to the cold shade of Opposition; for let it be remembered that the state of the House on that Friday night was a type of the real proportion of the two parties; or, in other words, that the Opposition, when they are all agreed, are two to one stronger than the party of the Government.

Mar. 27, 1858. Every one knows that Lord Palmerston has fallen, but no one who has not mixed with the parties in the House and heard the conversation of the Honourable Members can conceive to what a depth he has fallen. But lately he was the most popular Minister that England has had for many years; when he arose in the House cheers, long and loud, greeted him, and at his bidding 400 men at least would rush from all quarters of the kingdom to give him their support; but now he seems to be virtually deserted. The Tories of course rejoice, though with trembling, at his fall. The Whigs are sulky, and the Radicals are spitefully exultant. "We are in, it's true," say the Conservatives; "but! (with a significant shrug) it is all Palmerston's own fault," say the Whigs; whilst—"He is out, and serve him right," is the language of Radicals; and the "Great Minister," who but yesterday rode on the topmost crest of the waves of popularity, is sunk so low that there is hardly a man of his former friends to say, "God save him." Nor do men think of him in their speculations as to the future. That further changes are ahead every one believes, but nobody seems to imagine that Lord Palmerston can be reinstated.

CHAPTER VII.

THE INDIA BILL FOR THE REORGANISATION OF THE GOVERN-
MENT OF INDIA AFTER THE MUTINY—IT IS BROUGHT IN
BY MR. DISRAELI—PROVES AN UTTER FAILURE—LORD
JOHN RUSSELL'S RESOLUTION A SUCCESS—PROPERTY
QUALIFICATIONS AND MR. EDWARD AUCHMUTY GLOVER—
AN EXTRAORDINARY STORY.

April 3, 1858. ON Friday night Mr. Disraeli brought in
the India Bill. The House was crowded
by members, and every available place for strangers was
occupied. "Under the gallery" was filled by East India
directors, and the peers were down in unusual numbers.
Lord Ellenborough sat in the front. His Lordship
rarely appears in the House; indeed, we never saw him
there before. Mr. Disraeli began his speech about five
o'clock, and we have seldom found the House so silent
and attentive. Every word was distinct and clear as a bell
in the night. And no wonder. Mr. Disraeli had severely
criticised the Bill of the noble Lord opposite, little thinking
then that he would so soon occupy his great antagonist's
place, and himself be called upon to substitute a measure
for the one which he handled so unmercifully. And the
question, What will he do with the great Indian matter?
naturally excited the deepest interest. And, moreover,
though Mr. Disraeli introduced the measure into the House

of Commons, of course it was known that my Lord Ellenborough was the framer of the measure—the same Lord
Ellenborough who was once Governor-General in trying
times, who is generally considered a high authority on Indian
matters, and who has been held up by the late Sir Charles
Napier and others as an eminent statesman and one of the
few really great men who have been called to rule over our
Eastern possessions. But lately his Lordship was a severe
critic of the management of our Indian government; and to
the question, What will he do? men of all parties naturally
looked with great anxiety for an answer. It is not our
intention here to analyse the measure which has resulted
from the incubation of Lord Derby's Government. All we
can do is to show how it was received in the House. For
the most part, then, we have to report that it was received
with grim silence, and the only cheers came from the
Conservatives, who of course, as in duty bound, encouraged
their leader. But there was one exception, and that was
very laughable. We can easily conceive that there was
great anxiety in the Cabinet whilst the measure was under
consideration to give it a popular character. My Lord
Derby and his friends are Conservative, it is true, but the
cue is now to show that Conservatives are really the true
Liberals, and here was a fine opportunity to prove this to
the sceptical world, and it was with this view no doubt that
the principle of popular election was introduced. Lord
Palmerston's Bill gave the appointment of the Council to
the Crown, and caused great dissatisfaction in certain
quarters; let us step in advance of the noble Lord, and
show that *we* are not afraid of the application of the
representative principle even to the government of India."
At all events, it was quite clear by his manner of approach-
ing this part of the measure that Mr. Disraeli thought that
he was about to offer to the House and the country a

valuable *bonne bouche*, and it was clear that he expected
to be interrupted by loud cheers of delight as he unrolled
this part of the Indian charter. But, alas! it was not so—
for when he told the House that London would return one
member, instead of cheers there was solemn silence; when
he said Liverpool would send another, there was a low
murmur; when he proceeded to unfold the scroll further,
and reveal Glasgow returning another, the murmurs increased, mingled with signs of merriment; and when he
mentioned Belfast the House broke out into a regular
chorus of laughter. At this the Right Honourable Gentleman was evidently surprised, and we could fancy him
soliloquising thus: "Why, what would you have? When
I was a Conservative, I did not please you—and now that I
am 'coming the Liberal,' you laugh at me." Verily it is a
perverse generation. "I mourned with you, and you would
not lament; I pipe to you, and you will not dance." And
then there came another funny incident—certain gentlemen
are to be named in the Bill as members of the Council, and
the names of these the Chancellor of the Exchequer went
over with real solemnity, and when he came to Sir James
Hogg he paused, not being quite ready with the name of
the next, and at length said, to fill up the time, "the next
is a gentleman," and then paused again. At this the House
laughed uproariously. Sir James Hogg sat for many years
in the House, and was not remarkable for his urbanity, but
on the contrary; and this inference, which the words would
bear, that Sir James was not a gentleman, but that the next
was, tickled the House amazingly, and Mr. Disraeli added
to the fun by his unconsciousness of the cause of the
merriment. He seemed to think that the House was
laughing at the announcement of Sir James Hogg, and
began a defence of the Honourable Baronet; and then, of
course, to the surprise of the Right Honourable Gentleman,

the House laughed still more.   But we must leave off; the
general opinion in the House of the Bill is that "it won't
do."   This introduction of the principle of popular election
into the appointment of the executive is quite a new thing,
and at present no one seems to admire it.   And the question
of what the Government will do begins to agitate the Clubs:
will they alter the Bill—withdraw it—or press it to a division
and be defeated?   Perhaps the latter, and then go to the
country upon the measure.

April 24, 1858.   Edward Auchmuty Glover, late Member
of Parliament for Beverley, in Yorkshire,
has come to grief in a somewhat singular manner.   At
what time Mr. Glover first felt the stirrings of ambition to become a member of Parliament we have no
means of ascertaining, but he first came forward as a
candidate at the general election in 1857, when he defeated
Mr. William Wells by a majority of 42.   Beverley is an
open borough—one of those few places in the empire in
which there is no "predominant influence," and, therefore,
liable to the incursions of adventurers of the Glover sort.
What induced Mr. Glover to select Beverley, and how he,
without money or friends, succeeded in persuading the
worthy and independent electors thereof to elect him, is
unknown to us.   Suffice it to say that he was duly and truly
elected, and on the first day of the new Parliament's history
walked into the House of Commons a British senator.   It
was on that day he was pointed out to us as a somewhat
singular legislator, and one who our informant prophesied
would not for very long grace the House with his presence.
He is not a bad-looking man, this Mr. Glover, rather tall,
stoutly made, and, on the whole, of passable appearance.
He affected rather the swell—wore a hat with a curled brim,
and a rather ponderous watch-chain; but still there was

nothing especially singular in his appearance to make him a
prominent object among the crowds of new members who
poured into the House on that day. Reports, however, soon
began to be freely whispered that all was not right, and that
attempts would be made to oust him from a position which,
it was said with something of mystery, he was not worthy
to hold; and, when the time came, a petition was lodged
against him, complaining that Mr. Glover had obtruded
himself into this august assembly without the necessary
qualification—not the necessary qualification of mental and
educational fitness and experience, for of these matters the
Legislature takes no account. It makes candidates for
clerkships in the excise and other offices undergo a com-
petitive examination, but a legislator is not subjected to any
such test. One Mr. Livesay, of Preston, lately presented a
petition to the House, praying that all candidates for seats
in the House of Commons should undergo an examination;
but though it seems to be irrefragable in logic that if an
excise officer is required to prove that he is sufficiently
educated to gauge a cask or a malt-cistern, a man who
aspires to make our laws should prove, before competent
examiners, that he is educationally qualified for this somewhat more important duty. We have not come to that yet,
and Mr. Livesay's petition was only laughed at. At present,
if an Englishman be elected by the people, and have the
necessary property qualification—to wit, for a county £600 a
year, and for a borough £300—in every other particular he
is considered to be qualified to make our laws. The com-
plaint against Mr. Glover was that he had not the necessary
sum of £300 a year, and on this issue being heard before a
committee of the House, the decision was against him, and
his election was declared void. Now, in ordinary cases no
further proceedings are taken. The object is to get rid of
the sitting member, and, this being done, his opponents are

satisfied.   But Mr. Glover seems to have fallen into rough
hands, for, not satisfied with ousting him from Parliament,
they determined to prosecute him for making a false declaration, or, in other words, for swearing he was worth £300
a year, when he knew all the while he was not, and in due
time he was so prosecuted.   The fact was proved against
him to the satisfaction of a jury, and, alas! instead of lifting
up his head in Parliament, he is now in Newgate prison.
Poor Mr. Glover! when he set sail for the palace of Westminster with a fair wind, he little thought of landing
ultimately and so soon on such an inhospitable shore.
About twelve months ago he was chaired through the
streets of Beverley, and rapturously cheered by enthusiastic
crowds, and now he is in durance vile, with no man to do
him reverence.

Mr. Glover, then, is in Newgate, not for entering into
Parliament without a qualification, but for making a false
declaration, in that he declared before the authorities of the
House that he was possessed of £300 a year, whereas, at
the time that he so declared, he knew that he was not.
"But," it will probably be asked, "are there not many of
the other members who have made the declaration, who,
nevertheless, are really and truly and *bonâ fide* no more
qualified than Mr. Glover was?"   Well, probably there are;
indeed, unless rumour lie, there certainly are; but then, if
they had not a real qualification when they signed the
declaration, they had the show of one—they had one on
parchment if they had not the reality.   And this is the
difference between those gentlemen's cases and Mr. Glover's.
They, when they signed the declaration, had a deed in their
possession, for the time, which conveyed to them certain
lands or rent-charges, or other real or personal property,
and, if required, this deed·was produced and stopped all
questioning; but Mr. Glover had no such deed.   It is true

that these conveyances are all a sham; that really they do
not invest the possessor with a single farthing; that he
cannot take a penny of the estate so conveyed; and that,
in short, he is under solemn promise, and perhaps under a
bond, to re-convey as soon as the occasion has passed; but
still, according to the custom of the House, these deeds are
never questioned; and however notorious it may be that,
really and *bonâ fide*, the member has no other income than
that which he earns, if he produce one of these deeds he is
allowed to pass. "But is not this *morally* as bad as the
conduct of Mr. Glover?" Perhaps so, though into this
question we need not enter; but then as the law stands
it is not a crime, and we know the distinction between vice
and crime. Lord Lilburne, in Sir Bulwer-Lytton's novel of
"Night and Morning," admirably puts it: "Dykeman," said
he, "I know the law better than you can, for my whole life
has been spent in doing what I please without ever putting
myself in the power of LAW. You are right in saying
violence would be a capital crime. Now, the difference
between vice and crime is this: vice is what parsons write
sermons against—crime is what we make laws against.
Vices are safe things. I may have my vices like other men,
but crimes are dangerous things, illegal things, things to be
carefully avoided." Whether he who presents one of these
sham deeds is guilty of a vice we are not prepared to decide;
indeed, we decide nothing; but he is not guilty of a crime,
and Mr. Glover was. If Mr. Glover had borrowed a con-
veyance of a friend, he might have declared safely that he
was worth £300 a year and escaped Newgate, although
really he would not have been a penny richer than he is
now.

It is generally believed in the House that this prosecution
will prove the death-blow to property qualification. Members, especially those who got in by means of loaned

qualifications, evidently feel ashamed of this anomalous state of things. Here is a man in gaol for saying that he had £300 a year when he had not. There is a man who did the same in a different form, and he is addressing the House amidst rapturous cheers.

May 15, 1858. In an article which we published three weeks ago, we sketched the unfortunate career of Mr. Edward Auchmuty Glover, who, at the last general election, started for Beverley, was elected its representative in Parliament, unseated on petition alleging want of qualification, prosecuted for perjury by order of the House of Commons, and sentenced to imprisonment. Since the publication of this sketch we have received a communication from a relative of Mr. Glover on this subject, the substance of which we feel bound in justice to this unfortunate gentleman to lay before our readers. Mr. Glover, it appears from the communication, is not a mere adventurer, but a gentleman of an ancient and highly respectable Kentish family, tracing back to one John Glover, who bore the canopy as Baron of the Cinque Ports at the coronation of Henry VIII. He is also a Barrister-at-Law, Justice of the Peace for the county of Middlesex and city of Westminster, and F.G.S., F.S.A. And it is further stated that he is "an accomplished scholar, an eloquent speaker, and an elegant writer." With respect to his means and prospects, our correspondent tells us that his income "is never less than £1,500 a-year, derived from his own intellectual pursuits," that he has an estate in Ireland worth £6,000, mortgaged only for £1,400, and that he is heir to an estate valued at £47,000, and mortgaged for only £16,000. We have no time, space, or inclination to test or comment upon this statement. We leave it to make its own impression upon the minds of our readers—merely saying that we always

thought, and think still, that Mr. Glover was hardly dealt
with.

[The property qualification was immediately afterwards
abolished.]

CHAPTER VIII.

THE DEBATE ON LORD CANNING'S PROCLAMATION TO THE
LANDOWNERS OF OUDH AFTER THE INDIAN MUTINY—
MR. CARDWELL'S SPEECH—THE SUCCESS OF SIR HUGH
M. CAIRNS, AFTERWARDS LORD CAIRNS—MR. BRIGHT—
SIR JAMES GRAHAM—MR. DISRAELI—COLLAPSE OF THE
ATTACK ON THE GOVERNMENT.

May 14, 1858. THE excitement in the House and in the
Lobby, on Friday, the 14th, when the great
debate on Mr. Cardwell's motion began, was beyond
anything that we have seen in our time. That which
prevailed on the occasion of the Chinese debate, and the
battle for office when the Conspiracy Bill was discussed
and rejected, certainly did not come up to this. At half-
past three o'clock there was a large number of members
in the House, though the Speaker did not come in to
prayers until ten minutes to four; and at five o'clock, when
Mr. Cardwell rose to move his resolution, there could not
have been less than 550 members present. They filled all
the seats below, crowded the side galleries, and even then
many were obliged to stand clustering at the bar and behind
the Speaker's chair. For be it known that, notwithstanding
some million and a half of money has been spent on the
Westminster Palace, and the building covers several acres
of ground, " the House " is not large enough to seat all the
members. What is wanting is more room; and, if possible,

more room must be made, but as the Chamber is surrounded by solid stone walls some three feet in thickness, which form the main support of this part of the building, it will be exceedingly difficult, without incurring an enormous expense, to enlarge the area. In the outer Lobby there was so dense a crowd of strangers that the free ingress and egress of the members was seriously impeded, and access to the various offices in the Lobby was all but impossible. About 5.30, therefore, it was found necessary to clear the Lobby and drive all the strangers, much to their annoyance, into the distant Central Hall, where they waited and waited for hours in the vain hope of getting in to hear the debate, or, if that were impossible, to learn something of its progress and its probable results.

It was about five o'clock when Mr. Cardwell arose in his usual position below the gangway to bring forward his resolution, so portentous to the Derby Government. Mr. Cardwell is well known in the House, and has a high reputation there. He is the son of a Liverpool merchant, was educated at Oxford, where he took a double-first, and acted in Sir Robert Peel's Government as Secretary for the Treasury, and in the Earl of Aberdeen's as President of the Board of Control. Mr. Cardwell has been of late years ranked among the Peelites, but his prominence in the attack upon the Conservative Government seems to augur that if occasion offer he will join a Palmerstonian Ministry, whatever his old associates, Gladstone and Graham, may do. The perturbed spirit of Sir Robert Peel, represented by his followers, still haunts Mr. Disraeli with purpose of vengeance. In 1852, Gladstone, by his powerful speech upon the Budget, overthrew the Ministry, blighted Disraeli's opening prospects, and sent him back to the cold regions of Opposition. And now another Peelite confronts him, threatens to cut short his career of office, and nip in the bud his hopes of

at least attaining his pension of £2,000 a-year, which a few
more months' service would give him for life.   Mr. Cardwell's
speech was not a grand display.   The Right Hon. Gentleman, indeed, is not capable of anything of the sort.   He is
an able reasoner, but nothing more; he never attempts to
excite his audience; and his speech on Friday night, as the
opening speech in such a momentous debate, was hardly a
success.   His statements were clear, his reasoning cogent,
but he caused little excitement, and elicited little cheering.
Mr. Cardwell is unquestionably an able man, would make a
capital financial statement as Chancellor of the Exchequer,
and can expose and lay bare a fallacy as well as any man in
the House; but he is not an orator, and can hardly be called
eloquent.

"But see, Cairns is up; we will just stop and hear what
line of defence the Government mean to take, and then we
will go."   Such was the resolve uttered or silently made by
scores of honourable members, but it was not fulfilled—for
through another hour they sat in their places in spite of all
calls and cravings of appetite, however urgent, chained and
riveted by Sir Hugh's masterly speech.   The Right Honourable Gentleman took everybody by surprise that night.   He
has been in Parliament since 1852, when he was returned
for Belfast, and during this short parliamentary career he
had gradually come to be looked upon as a rising man, and
"booked certain" for a place if the Conservatives should
come into power.   As a speaker he had the reputation of
being a clear and able debater in legal matters, but nothing
more.   But now it appears that he only wanted the occasion
to show he could be more than that.   On Friday he had the
occasion.   He no longer stood below the gangway of the
Opposition of the House, but on the Ministerial bench, her
Majesty's Solicitor-General, and selected by his colleagues
to lead the van in the defence of the Government in peril.

And it is saying but little that he was equal to the occasion, for he was more than that. His speech, for these degenerate days, was a great and successful effort, and for the time Sir Hugh was completely master of the situation, and all that Cardwell and Deasy had uttered was forgotten for the time and clean gone from our minds. The cheering of the Conservatives was vociferous, almost beyond all precedent; many of the Radicals joined in the applause, and not even the oldest of the Whig opponents could refuse to award to him their meed of praise. But it could not be said of Sir Hugh as it was once said of Fox, after one of his orations :—

> " So charming was his voice, that we awhile
> Thought him still speaking, still stood fixed to hear."

For no sooner had the Right Hon. Gentleman sat down than the House arose, as if impelled by some common motive power suddenly brought to bear, and rushed off to dinner; and in three minutes from the time that the Solicitor-General sat down, four hundred members had streamed out, leaving only some hundred or less behind to doze upon the benches under the soothing eloquence of Mr. Robert Lowe. And now for two hours, as usual, all was quiet. No cheers or noise of any kind arose, but solemn silence reigned. A few minutes ago the House was a vortex of excitement, now it is like a city church on a Sunday afternoon, when a dull, prosy preacher addresses a sparse and somnolent congregation. We confess ourselves to a comfortable nap on the occasion. For some time we kept our eyes upon the white head of the Right Hon. Member for Kidderminster, and our ears open to listen to his arguments, but gradually our winking eyelids closed, our senses wandered. We thought we were looking at a dissolving view. The House seemed to change into a leafy wood, and then we were lying by the side of a trickling stream on a

hot summer day. How long we continued in this Elysium
we know not, but when we awoke the House was rapidly
filling, and Mr. Vernon Smith was upon his legs. Of course
we roused ourselves at once, and called back our scattered
senses, for we knew that there was fun to be expected.

Mr. Vernon Smith is not generally a commanding speaker;
and on ordinary occasions we should have been quite contented to sleep on; but we knew that on this occasion
he would be worth listening to, for he had to explain how
it was that a certain letter which he had received from Lord
Canning had not been sent on to his successor, Lord Ellenborough. The history of this notable letter is of course
known to our readers. It came by the same mail which
brought over Lord Canning's celebrated proclamation, and
contained a paragraph referring to that proclamation, and
promising all explanations by the next mail. The proclamation went to the President of the Board of Control, and
the letter which promised the explanation Mr. Vernon
Smith kept in his pocket; and it was alleged that if Lord
Ellenborough had known that such a promise had been
received he would not have sent his questionable despatch
until this explanation had been forthcoming. The Ministerial side of the House was uncommonly excited when Mr.
Vernon Smith arose, for a suspicion had become prevalent
that this letter was purposely withheld—that, in fact, the
keeping it back was an artifice planned by Mr. Vernon
Smith and Lord Palmerston to embarrass the Government.
When, therefore, Mr. Vernon Smith alluded to this letter,
it was no marvel that the Ministerial side of the House was
in an uproar. For a time the Right Hon. Member could
hardly be heard. Shouts of " Oh! oh!" "Read! read!"
met every attempt at explanation; and when he became
excited, and defiantly cried out, " No, I cannot read it," the
storm was terrific, and for a time you could no more hear

what the Right Hon. Gentleman was saying than you could hear a bird piping near the Niagara Falls. We tried to analyse the noise, but found it impossible. There were shouts of "Read! read!" long-drawn groans of contempt and execration, and sharp cries of "Oh! oh!" as if the utterers were astounded, whilst others expressed their feelings by cries which are not repeatable on paper, simply because we cannot spell them. But the climax came when Mr. Vernon Smith denounced the charge that he had been influenced by factious motives in withholding that letter as "a falsehood." Matters began to look serious then. In the House of Commons you may insinuate that an opponent has told a fib, and you may prove it by the most convincing logic, so that every man in the House may see that there is no escape from the deduction that he has really been guilty of untruth; all this is parliamentary—but you must not give the lie direct. When, therefore, Mr. Vernon Smith used the word "falsehood," as we have said, matters looked serious. The groans and other noises were changed at once into shouts of "order," and Mr. Lygon, a young Conservative, leaped up to demand an explanation of the word. Mr. Disraeli also arose, and for a minute or so there were three members on their legs at once, confronting each other. This, of course, was extremely disorderly; and in the late Speaker's reign he would have risen, put down Mr. Lygon and Mr. Disraeli, and called upon Mr. Smith to retract; but the present Speaker seemed disposed to allow the members "to fight it out" among themselves, for he neither arose nor made sign. Mr. Lygon, when he saw the Leader of the House was up, sat down. Mr. Disraeli "was sure the Right Hon. Gentleman," &c., &c.; Mr. Vernon Smith, of course, "did not intend to use the word offensively," &c., &c., and so the matter passed off. But we must leave Mr. Vernon Smith, perhaps never to notice him again; for if the auguries are to be relied upon, the official career of the gentleman is closed. At all events, he did not add to his reputation nor brighten his prospects by this display.

We had no speaking after this worth notice until Lord John Russell arose. Lord John's rising was the signal for every member to take his place and attentively listen. For though rumour had for several days foretold that on this occasion the noble Lord would "go against the Government," yet all were anxious to have assurance made doubly sure by his Lordship's own avowal. For Lord John still has a tail of followers, somewhat shortened, perhaps, of late, but sufficiently long to make his decision in such a battle as this a matter of great importance. The noble Lord did not leave the House long in doubt, if any doubt had been entertained. He supports Mr. Cardwell's motion, and if the Government fall there can hardly be a question that Lord John will be a prominent member of the next Cabinet. When the noble Lord sat down the House had evidently "had enough of it." For seven hours it had been in debate, and when Mr. Roebuck moved the adjournment all parties joyfully assented. Mr. Speaker put the question, and again the members rushed out like a torrent, and in a few minutes all this wild scene had vanished like a phantasmagoria.

On Monday night the desire to get into the House was as strong as ever, for it was thought that this would be the great night, but it did not prove so. The great night, when Gladstone, Graham, Bright, Palmerston, and Disraeli will address the House, will be Thursday or Friday. On Monday we had Roebuck (who opened the ball), Sir Charles Wood, and Mr. Whiteside. Roebuck did not speak with his usual vigour; he has been an invalid of late. Sir Charles Wood, under the influence of the bracing air of the Opposition side of the House, was unusually lively; and Mr. Whiteside " performed," as he always does, with immense energy. Oh! there was Sir Robert Peel; we must not ignore the gay and gallant Sir Robert. The House does not, for whenever it is known that he is about to speak the House always fills, for if there is not much to be learned there is always something to be laughed at. And it is, moreover, worth something to see Sir Robert address the House of Commons. His fine commanding person, his perfect ease, and his appropriate and elegant action, are what you do not see often, and certainly cannot be found united in any other speaker. Of his speeches themselves we have not much to say of a laudatory kind, but the "settings" are certainly very remarkable.

Never in our time has there been so much uncertainty about the result of a fierce parliamentary battle. Usually the "Whips" can make up their books with tolerable accuracy, but we do not believe that in this instance any one can calculate where the end will be. At first there seemed to be no doubt that the Government would be beaten, but its prospects have certainly brightened within the last forty-eight hours. The attack upon Mr. Vernon Smith has been exceedingly damaging to the Opposition. Private letters, too, it is said, have been received from Sir Colin Campbell and General Outram condemning Lord Canning's proclamation, and Saturday's provincial papers have shown to many Liberal members that their constituencies are not so zealous to bring back a Palmerston Government as they were supposed to be; and on the whole we are disposed to estimate the chances of a Government victory much higher than we did at the close of the debate on Friday night. On Tuesday night a change had manifestly come over both parties. The Liberals looked apprehensive, the Conservatives looked hopeful, and towards the close of the night it was confidently stated that the Opposition would make a merit of necessity and follow the example of the Government, and accept Mr. Dillwyn's amendment. The debate, it is said, will not finish until Friday night, or rather Saturday morning. Graham and Gladstone and Bright and Palmerston and Disraeli have yet to speak. How it will all end it is impossible to say, but there are certainly signs of the storm passing over.

May 29, 1858. The great fight is over. It was a drawn battle, equivalent to a disastrous defeat of the Whigs, and better than a victory to the Government. We resume our account of "the great debate." Lord Goderich by right opened the ball on Thursday night. The Noble Lord moved the adjournment on Tuesday, and by parliamentary rule it devolved upon him to begin the debate on Thursday. Lord Goderich is the eldest son of the Earl of Ripon (the Prosperity-Robinson of former days), and heir to the earldom. He came into Parliament in 1852 for Hull; he afterwards sat for Huddersfield, and last year succeeded Cobden as member for the West Riding. The Noble Lord holds Radical opinions—believes in extension of the suffrage, short parliaments, and vote by ballot; hence his success in his electioneering career, for, as Coppock used to say, " a lord is always formidable, but a Radical lord is irresistible." But, in addition to these sources of the noble Lord's popularity, he possesses considerable ability, and in private life is a very estimable character. He is the intimate friend of Carlyle, an active coadjutor of Maurice in all his projects for the elevation of working men, and takes a deep interest in the social questions of the day. It will be remembered that in a dispute between the " Amalgamated Engineers " and their employers he was chosen by the working men to represent their interests. Lord Goderich is a good speaker—always gets up his case carefully, and but for a fatal defect in his voice, which is thin, and wants power,

would be able to address the House with great effect. His
speech on Thursday night was a very successful effort. It
was highly praised by the Opposition, and listened to with
great respect by the adherents of the Government. If the
Whigs had succeeded in overthrowing the Ministry, it is
more than probable that Lord Goderich would have been in-
cluded in the next administration. Some people have argued
from this that Lord Goderich has narrowed his views of late,
thrown over the Radical and adopted the Whig formula; but
we do not know that we have any right to infer this, for it
was acknowledged that the expected Liberal Ministry was to
be formed upon a wider basis than the last; was to be, in
short, what has been humorously called a " Broad-bottomed
Government." Lord Goderich spoke before dinner, and
when he sat down there were the usual symptoms of a
break-up; members looked at the clock; some rose to go;
others were actually on the move; but in the midst of the
bustle and noise, the cheers for Lord Goderich, and the
movements of those who were anxious for dinner, a portly
form is seen to arise from the second seat below the gangway on the Opposition side of the House and front the
Speaker. It was John Bright, and at once the buzzing
and shuffling and disturbance were quelled. Those who
had risen sat down; those who had left their places sidled
noiselessly back again; and every man prepared himself to
listen with attention to what was coming. But much effort
to listen is not required when Bright is speaking. There
needs no stretching out of the neck, no sheltering the ear
with the hand to concentrate the sound; every man may
sit at his ease, whether he be behind or above, or at a distance from the orator. Bright's voice, strong, clear, and
musical, will be sure to reach the listener wherever he is,
and every word will fall upon the ear distinct and well
defined. Bright has the best voice in the House of Com-

mons. Its keynote is about lower G in the tenor clef, and he seldom modulates it more than half a note higher or lower. Some speakers in the House, Sir Bulwer-Lytton, for instance, take the range of an octave—at one time shrieking in alto and the next moment groaning in the bass; but Bright never rises or falls more than half a note, and seldom so much as that—hardly enough, we should say, to give due force and expression to what he utters. This slight fault arises, we have no doubt, from Bright's early practice of speaking to large assemblies out-of-doors in the great Anti-Corn Law struggle, when it was absolutely necessary to keep the voice up to a certain pitch in order to make the people hear. Indeed, we are not sure that the same necessity is not felt in the House of Commons, for when this chamber is full it is not a good place to speak in. Very few of the prominent speakers are successful in the modulation of their voices. Whiteside and Bulwer-Lytton are extravagant; Disraeli is perhaps the most accomplished in the art; and next to him Gladstone.

But enough of this. Bright's speech was a startler; there has been nothing like it in the House in our time. On the Indian subject he said but little more than had been said by others; it was when he came to look at this battle from another standpoint that he produced the most effect. When he exposed the attack upon the Ministry as a party move; audaciously laid bare the *arcana* of the Opposition; the charms and the incantations practised by the hierophants of Whig mysteries; called attention to the indirect offers of places; showed how " beautifully engraved cards, inviting doubtful Liberals to splendid mansions, had been scattered wide, but with a discriminating hand," and contrasted the efforts of Rarey, who, in taming horses, appeals to the nobler instincts of the animal, with the leaders of the Opposition, who, in taming the refractory Liberals of No.

11, appealed to instincts of quite a contrary nature. There was one part of Bright's speech on this subject which produced an uproar positively frightful. And well it might, for surely nothing more scathing was ever uttered in Parliament. " If," said the Honourable Member, " those cards of invitation could give to the honourable members who received them the exact meaning of the senders, they would say, ' We have measured your heads, we have gauged your souls, and we believe that your character in this House will go for nothing in your estimation if you do but receive this miserable ' " invitation, we suppose the Honourable Gentleman said, but the last word was lost in the wild storm of oh's ! and groans which broke from the Opposition, and the laughter and uproarious cheering with which the Conservatives replied, and at length overwhelmed the indignant cries of the Whigs. For several minutes the storm raged. Not even when he ventured into the agricultural districts to advocate Free Trade did the Honourable Member for Birmingham ever invoke a more furious tempest. But calm and unmoved he stood until it subsided. We may here remark that the Conservatives beat the Liberals all hollow at a cheer. The reason, we fancy, is, there are more genuine country gentlemen in their ranks—men used to give the halloo in the hunting-fields. Your successful manufacturer and merchant hunts occasionally, no doubt, but such men are only amateurs, and not " to the manner born " ; while that middle-aged gentleman opposite, with the broad chest and wiry limbs, narrow-brimmed hat, and closely fitting coat, rode to cover when his legs could scarcely reach the bottom of the saddle flap, and see with what a will and how scientifically, with hand to his mouth, he is cheering. Perhaps, too, the firmness with which he holds to his political creed accounts for the heartiness of his cheering, for we have noticed, or think we have, that the Conservative gentleman

believes in his formula with a stronger faith than the
Liberal does in his. Your Liberal is generally a mere
dilettante in politics. His creed is often assumed for a
purpose, or is at best an opinion formed upon logical deduc-
tions; but the Tory country gentleman's has been received
from his ancestors, and is part of his very being.

Sir James Graham did not rise immediately after Bright,
for the dinner-hour had come, and the bulk of the members
rushed out of the House, leaving it to third-rate orators to
try their powers; just as we have seen at Lord's Cricket-
ground, when the "Marylebone" and "All England" go to
the tent to dine, the bat and ball are taken by standers-by
or underlings, who get up a little game amongst themselves
by way of practice. But about nine o'clock the House was
once more full, and then, having a "fit audience," the old
"Knight of Netherby" arose. Nothing could be a greater
contrast than Sir James's speech was to that of Bright.
The Honourable Member for Birmingham's was dashing;
the Right Honourable Member for Carlisle's was smashing.
Lord Derby, when Lord Stanley, was called the "Rupert of
debate"; Sir James may be likened to Cromwell's Iron-
sides—somewhat slow, heavily armed, but irresistible, clearing his way as he marched on with ponderous strength, and
bearing down all before him. Sir James never essays
oratorical flights, uses no rhetorical ornaments or flourishes,
is neither witty nor humorous, and seldom provokes a
laugh, but sets calmly to work to demolish his opponent's
arguments, and overwhelm him by a concentrated force of
facts. In person Sir James is tall and bulky, with strongly
marked features, and his style is singularly terse and clear.
We should say that, as a debater, he is supreme in the
House of Commons, and there is no man whom we would
rather have on our side than Sir James. He talked on this
occasion of his "shattered nerves," but he manifested no

signs of either mental or physical failure. On the contrary,
we thought this speech was one of his most vigorous and
characteristic efforts. The effect that it had upon the
House was very powerful. Sir Richard Bethell arose when
Sir James sat down, but with all his acknowledged talents
in debate, stimulated by the hope of the Great Seal, which
appeared to be within his reach, he was no match for the
stalwart Knight of Netherby. When Sir Richard finished
the debate closed, with the understanding that it was to
come to an end on the morrow. But who can ever know
what will be on the morrow? Prophecies without number had been uttered about the event of to-morrow, and
thousands of pounds had been laid upon the division, but
the prophecies all failed, and the bets were all off.

And yet on Thursday night we got some inkling of what
was coming. The coming event certainly sent its shadow
before, though that shadow was faint and undefined. It
was about eleven o'clock, or it might be half-past, when a
sagacious M.P. whispered in our ears, "It will all end in
smoke." "How?" said we. "I know not," he replied,
" but there seems to be some solvent at work that is rapidly
disintegrating the Opposition." And on close observation
we discovered something of this sort ourselves. Liberal
members were discoursing anxiously in knots, and indecision
and perplexity were marked in their faces. The Palmerstonian thermometer was evidently falling, and every one
acknowledged that the prospect of success was nothing like
so bright as it had been. At one time the Palmerstonians
boasted of a majority of 80, but now they only " hoped to
have at least 25." The activity of the " Whips " had been
extraordinary, and especially on the Government side. It
was said that there were 620 members in town. Faces
were seen in the House that had not appeared for months.
Bearded gentlemen, tanned by travel in foreign climes, had

heard the bruit of war in Germany, Italy, and France, and hurried home as fast as steam could bring them. Gentlemen who had been long confined at home by some accident hobbled into the House on crutches, and old men, who it was thought would never show up again, suddenly made their appearance. Still, on reflection, we could hardly see where the Government majority was to come from. And so matters stood when we retired from the House on Thursday night.

On Friday night the House met as usual at four o'clock. And never were members more devotional than on that occasion, for there were at least two hundred at prayers. (*Mem.* Unless a member be in the House at the time of prayers he cannot secure his seat for the evening.) About five o'clock, when the private business was finished, the House was densely crowded with members, as was also the lobby with strangers. The great, important day was come, big with the fate of the Derby Government. Within the next twelve hours much was to be decided. The question whether a Tory Government in England is possible was to be settled, and other questions of no mean importance to those immediately concerned—questions of salary, pensions, and patronage. " Will my quarter's salary come in full ? " " Shall I attain to that comfortable pension ? " " Will my brother get his step in the Guards ? or my cousin his living ? " &c. It was an agitating time, but not for long, for at 5.30 there arose from his seat below the gangway a member named Clay, the Radical member for Hull, to speak on the motion for the adjournment of the House. At first he attracted but little notice, and was scarcely heard amidst the buzz of conversation which was going on. But gradually the House became silent, for it discovered that Mr. Clay was making a singular request to Mr. Cardwell to withdraw his motion. Young and inex-

perienced members of the Liberal party laughed at the proposition, and cried indignantly, "No! no! Withdraw?
Why should he withdraw when he has a large majority at
his back?" But the "old birds" saw at once that "the
beginning of the end" was come, and that Mr. Clay was
only opening a farce, the programme of which was pre-
arranged. Nor did Mr. Cardwell's refusal surprise them.
"Of course, like a coy lady, he must refuse at first. But
you will see," said one of these old birds, "Palmerston will
arise soon and ask him to withdraw, and then he will con-
cur. It is settled, you may depend upon it." And so it
turned out. One after another hon. members arose and
reiterated the request, and then Mr. Cardwell sat still until
at length the time had come. Lord Palmerston slid into his
place from behind the Speaker's chair, and said, "that as
the despatches which had been laid upon the table had
somewhat changed the aspect of affairs, &c., and as the
House seemed to wish it, he would recommend his Right
Hon. Friend to withdraw his motion." And then Mr.
Cardwell arose, and, of course, "in compliance with the
wishes of the House, reluctantly consented." And the
battle which for a fortnight past had agitated the nation was
over, and nothing now remained but that Mr. Disraeli should
perform his part in the farce, and give his consent to the
withdrawal; and so, when Mr. Cardwell sat down, Mr.
Chancellor of the Exchequer arose.

This was really, perhaps, the proudest moment of Disraeli's life. Only last night he was hemmed in by an army
of fierce and apparently relentless foes, determined upon
his destruction. And now that army is all broken up,
demoralised, and sueing at his hands for permission to
depart.

And if Disraeli's position was a proud one, how mortifying must have been Cardwell's and Palmerston's! They

confidently reckoned upon victory, and had, in anticipation, divided the spoil, and lo! instead thereof they are obliged to surrender without a battle. In "Tancred" Mr. Disraeli makes his hero say, when he meditates a journey to Jerusalem: "I go to a land which has never been blessed with that fatal drollery, a representative government." As the noble Lord walked moodily home on that night we should not be surprised if he were disgusted with this "fatal drollery." Oh, for the old days of party, when there were no "independent members who cannot be depended upon."

June 3, 1858. Touching the excise duty on paper, let us relate a remarkable fact germane to the matter. Some years ago there was a duty on paper-hangings of 25 per cent.: that is to say, on paper-hangings at 6d. a yard the duty was 1½d., on paper-hangings at 1s. per yard the duty was 3d. Well, when the duty existed, and up to the time when it was abolished, the lowest-priced paper that was manufactured was sold at 4d. per yard, and it might have been supposed that the removal of this duty would reduce the common paper-hangings about 1d., or say 1½d. But what is the fact? Why, you can buy now a far better paper at 1d. per yard. The cause of this extraordinary fall in price is, first, the removal of the duty from the paper; but, secondly, and chiefly, the removal of the exciseman from the premises of the manufacturer. Let statesmen ponder this remarkable fact. Mr. Milner Gibson has once more brought the odious paper-tax under the consideration of Parliament, and this time he has succeeded in obtaining its condemnation from the House of Commons. If the Whigs had been in power it is questionable whether he would have attained his object; for Lord Palmerston would have resisted the motion, and at the ring of the bell some hundred members, albeit they had not

heard a word of the debate, would have rushed up from the re-
freshment-rooms wiping their lips, or from the smoking-room
all redolent of tobacco, to support their chief. But the bonds
of party are happily, for a time, broken. The great Liberal
body no longer look through party spectacles, but with
unglazed eyes; they vote according to the dictates of reason,
and not as they are bidden. Mr. Disraeli knows this. He
can, in a measure, command the minority — he cannot,
however, command it as despotically as Palmerston; but he
cannot rule the majority opposite, and so on this subject, as
he has done on many others, he wisely gave way. A weak
Government doubtless has its evils; but it is questionable
whether a strong Government, with a blind unreasoning
majority at its back, does not lead to worse.

CHAPTER IX.

LORD STANLEY—PROFESSOR BLACKIE—BARON ROTHSCHILD SWORN AT LAST.

June 10, 1858. DURING the last week or two Lord Stanley has been the real leader of the House, for the business of the House has been the discussion of the India Bill, and of course Lord Stanley, as President of the Board of Control, has taken the lead in this discussion. It had long been a settled point in the House of Commons that Lord Stanley must soon take some high office. It did not seem possible that a nobleman of such high birth and connections and un-questionable talents should remain much longer out of power. But though this was settled, it illustrates the curious state of parties in the House ; these men had by no means made up their minds as to which section of the House the noble lord would join. He sat on the Conserva-tive side, below the gangway ; but every speech that he delivered seemed to prove that he was more of a philosophic Radical than a Conservative. Some of his speeches were denounced by Spooner and Bentinck, *et hoc genus omne,* as positively shocking for their latitudinarian spirit; and we confess that if Lord Stanley had eschewed office altogether

for the present, and placed himself at the head of the
Radicals, we should not have been surprised. Lord Palmerston, it is clear, did not consider that the noble Lord was
irrevocably pledged to the Conservative party, for in 1855,
on the death of Sir William Molesworth, he invited Lord
Stanley to succeed Sir William as Secretary for the
Colonies. But, however, here he is sitting, not as the leader
of the Radicals, nor as Secretary for the Colonies with the
Whigs, but as President of the Board of Control in a
Conservative Ministry. Nevertheless, though he has
joined the Conservative Government, and sits on the
Ministerial bench, we venture to say that Lord Stanley
is not a Conservative. Neither is he a Whig; certainly not.
Nor do we think that we can designate him as a Radical.
Indeed, we doubt whether he holds to any well-defined
political formula. He is, in our opinion, a calm, philo-
sophical statesman, and will not be found, in the long run,
giving to party what is meant for mankind. Under the old
political *régime*, when every member of a ministry was
obliged on all questions to follow the leader, we doubt
whether Lord Stanley could have joined any ministry, and
certainly not a Conservative Government. But the old
political *régime* has passed away; the despotism of the
Prime Minister is nothing like what it used to be; strict
party questions have become much fewer in number; much
greater latitude of action is allowed; and " open questions "
are every day growing more common. Hence it is that
men of many different opinions on important political
subjects find it possible to serve in the same Cabinet.
Lord Stanley is a young man to take so high an office as
President of the Board of Control. He is thirty-two years
old this year. In person he is rather tall, and he is very
different in appearance from the bearded and moustached
scions of noble houses who lounge about the lobby. He

wears no hair on his face, dresses neatly, and affects no finery. His associates seem to be few in number, for he is seldom seen in company with any one, but marches through the lobby alone, unnoticed by any one, and noticing no one as he passes—evidently, a silent, retiring man. The noble Lord has a good forehead, prominent and lofty, and a remarkably serious and thoughtful face. The speeches of Lord Stanley are always good and always listened to, and he frequently throws out thoughts which are worth remembering; but his delivery is ineffective, and always must be so, owing to some fault in his voice, the cause of which we have never been able to discover. Some say that he has a defective roof of the mouth, others say that he is what is popularly called short-tongued; but we do not think so. The defect is simply a thickness of utterance, but whether this arises from some faulty construction of the speaking organs, or from a bad habit early contracted, we are not able to say.

In the Lobby of the House of Commons one morning, when the Scotch University Bill was on, there appeared a stranger, who not only received considerable attention from the Scotch members, but attracted a good deal of observation generally. He was rather a short man, with a sharp, lively, restless face, closely shaven, long white hair which almost reached his shoulders, and a merry, twinkling eye, which age has not yet dimmed. His dress was not singular, excepting his broad-brimmed hat. In his hand he carried a formidable cane with a heavy ivory hook. This gentleman was Professor Blackie, Professor of Greek, we believe, in the Edinburgh University, who was elected some time ago by the Town Council, by a majority of one, to succeed Professor Dunbar, just then deceased. Professor Blackie had, of course, come up to town to watch this new Bill, which is intended to shake up the seats of learning in the

North from the lethargy into which they had fallen, and
reform them altogether. But the Professor had not come,
like some of his brethren, in fear of the measure, but rather
in hope that it may open up a new era for Scottish education; for Mr. Blackie is an ardent reformer, and by his
lectures and writings has loudly proclaimed the fact that the
Scottish Universities have dropped behind the age, and
warmly preached the necessity of reform.

The great event came off on Monday—the
admission of Baron Rothschild to take his
seat at last as a member of the House of Commons.   It
was managed in the manner following : — The   Bill
received   the   Royal   assent   on   Friday,   and,   as   no
notice appeared on the paper on Monday that Lord
John Russell would move the necessary resolution to
enable the Baron to take his seat, only a few who were
in the secret knew that the Honourable Member would
present himself on that day.   But the fact is, as was
satisfactorily settled by a conclave of authorities, this is a
case of privilege and therefore no notice is necessary.
And so on Monday morning, as soon as the House opened,
Baron Rothschild presented himself at the bar, flanked on
one side by Lord John Russell and on the other by Mr.
John Abel Smith ; and Mr. Speaker seeing them, called out,
" Members who wish to be sworn come to the table."
Whereupon the Baron, attended as aforesaid, marched to
the bar, and the clerk presented to him the usual oath,
when up rose Mr. Warren, who was determined to protest
once more against this profanation of the House ; but he
was rebuked by the Speaker, who ruled that no interruption
to a member's taking the oath could be allowed.   The
Baron, of course, refused to take the customary oath, and
was ordered by the Speaker to withdraw below the bar, and

July 31, 1858.

Lord John Russell immediately arose and proposed the following resolution :—

"That it appears to this House that Baron Lionel Nathan de Rothschild, a person professing the Jewish religion, being otherwise entitled to sit and vote in this House, is prevented from so sitting and voting by his conscientious objection to take the Oath which by an Act passed in the present session of Parliament has been substituted for the Oaths of Allegiance, Supremacy, and Abjuration in the form therein required."

And here Mr. Warren, impatient not to lose his chance, once more attempted to speak, but on its being pointed out to him that this resolution was only declaratory, he again curbed his impatience and sat down, and the resolution passed *nem. con.*, and Lord John proceeded to propose resolution No. 2, to wit :—

"That any person professing the Jewish religion may henceforth, in taking the Oath prescribed in an Act of the present session of Parliament to entitle him to sit and vote in this House, omit the words, 'and I make this declaration upon the true faith of a Christian.' "

On the question being put, Mr. Warren unburthened his conscience. He was followed by Mr. Newdegate and Mr. Spooner, who also opposed the resolution, and by Mr. Walpole, who refused to offer any further opposition, and the House having divided and passed the resolution by 69 to 37, the Baron again, amidst loud cheering, walked to the table, and was sworn on the Old Testament in the manner prescribed. And so this great question, which has been agitated for eleven years, was settled. In conclusion, let the reader note that Lord John Russell's resolution does not merely cover Baron Rothchild's admission, but the admission of all Jews, and is therefore a standing order of the House. The House was thinly attended, and no Jews were present but Baron Rothchild's family. Even Alderman Salomons was not present. He meant to be there, but knew nothing about the matter until he arrived in London from his country seat at Tunbridge. He jumped into a hansom as soon as he heard of it, but arrived too late.

CHAPTER X.

Mar. 5, 1859. IT is impossible to let the episode of Mr.
Warren's farewell pass by without notice. It
was so characteristic of the House and the man. Mr.
Samuel Warren is an egotist of somewhat inflated proportions. When he entered the House in 1856 he was
solemnly impressed by the greatness of the event. When
he began life he little thought of being a member of
Parliament; and lo! here he is. He can enter that sacred
door without let or hindrance. His letters are addressed
"Samuel Warren, Esq., M.P." He is an "honourable
member," has a voice in the Imperial Legislature, and
through that voice can influence the policy of the world.
Nor, perhaps, did he deem the event less important in
parliamentary history than it was in his own. He was the
author of "Ten Thousand a-Year," "The Diary of a
Physician," which had sold by thousands, a work on
elections, &c., and Recorder of Hull. If he received honour
he also conferred it. And when, through dire necessity, he
was obliged to retire from the House, he felt it to be
impossible that *his* retirement should pass without notice.
Ordinary members in considerable numbers leave the

House as quietly as a cloud dissolves, but he was not an ordinary member. He must explain, bid the House and Speaker farewell, and, in short, have a scene—or, as an Hon. Member expressed it, go off, like a firework, with a bang. And then, in addition to Mr. Warren's egotism, we must also remember that Mr. Warren is a novelist, and that it is natural for novelists, and especially that class to which Mr. Warren belongs, to look upon the common transactions of life with a novelist's eye. Mr. Warren did so in his own case. His entrance into Parliament was the beginning of an episode in the story of his life, his parliamentary career was its progress, and his retirement its *dénouement;* and of course this must be made effective. He would explain—he would perorate—he would bid a solemn farewell to Mr. Speaker and the House—and then, in a grand Roman way, retire. Thursday, the 24th ult., was the day fixed for the solemn scene; and on Thursday Mr. Warren, who had been absent ever since he received the offer of place, walked into the House and took his accustomed seat, duly primed for the coming event. The House was unusually full that night, and during the preliminary business of presenting petitions and asking questions was noisy and restless — but this was nothing uncommon. "It will soon be quiet," doubtless thought Mr. Warren, "when I arise." And, of course, according to the novelist's rule, it ought to have been not only quiet but reverential; and, after attentively listening, should have greeted the retiring Member, as he marched out of the House, with a hearty farewell cheer. But the novelist's rules do not always hold good in actual life, as Mr. Warren soon discovered, doubtless to his great chagrin. The time at length came. Mr. Warren's name was called by the Speaker—for he had a notice upon the paper—and he arose. But, alas! the House was not reverential—not even

decently quiet. On the contrary, it seemed to us that the
buzz became louder, and the members more uneasy. On
the Treasury Bench the Ministers were in eager talk; on
the opposite side Lord Palmerston was chatting with Sir
Charles Wood. At the bar a crowd of members were
buzzing, and laughing, and joking; and everywhere honourable gentlemen were flitting about as if business had been
suspended. Mr. Warren of course went through his task;
he tried to lift himself up to the "height of his great
argument." He put on his solemnest manner and spoke
in his most serious tones; alas! to no effect. In short, the
scene was a failure, and, instead of Mr. Warren going off,
like a firework, with a bang, he was fain to die away like a
snuff of a candle. He spoke for some twenty minutes, but
what he said no one knew, and when he had finished he
slipped out by a side door without the faintest cheer to greet
him. Indeed, few people knew that he was gone until the
clerk's voice was heard calling on the next notice. Now,
all this might have been foretold by any one who knows the
House of Commons. This is not a Roman Senate, Mr.
Warren, but an English House of Commons, not fond of
display and characteristically intolerant of scenes. If you
had been shot in the lobby you might have been the subject
of a passing notice, but even then probably all that would
have been done would have been to order an investigation,
and the House would have calmly proceeded with its
business, like that cool gentleman that Mathews used to talk
about, who, when his wife was reduced by spontaneous com-
bustion to ashes whilst sitting at the dinner-table, merely
cried out, " Here, John, bring fresh glasses, and sweep
away your mistress." The last solemn scene in the House,
and the only one in our time, occurred when Peel died.
Then the House was deeply affected, and, to show its
respect for the great statesman, adjourned for several days;

but between Samuel Warren and Sir Robert Peel there is a wide difference, which fact Mr. Warren forgot. But, as an Hon. Member said, Warren is a good fellow, nevertheless, and clever too; and this is true, and in his prosperity we rejoice, and wish him long life to enjoy his salary. That he will do his duty in his new position ably and well we have not a doubt; and so farewell, Mr. Warren, and hearty good wishes.

Mar. 19, 1859. There are two Mr. Kinglakes in the House; both are named Alexander, and both are barristers by profession. One is named Alexander William, and the other John Alexander, but it is the former whom we have now to notice. John Alexander is Mr. Serjeant Kinglake, who is now a barrister in considerable practice. Alexander William gave up his practice, which was never large, in 1856. He and his kinsman came into Parliament in 1857—the Sergeant for Rochester, his cousin for Bridgewater. Mr. Serjeant Kinglake is noted only as a successful lawyer, but Mr. Alexander William Kinglake has achieved a widespread reputation as an author, although he has published but one volume, and that not a large one. It is, however, though small in volume, a great book, and has already become one of the classics of our language. Mr. Eöthen Kinglake (for so he is now pretty generally called) is a man of rather singular appearance, but we know not that he would have attracted notice here had not his fame as a writer preceded him. He is rather under the middle height, wears a formidable moustache, and large, round, powerfully-magnifying spectacles. When we first saw him we were obliged to confess to a disappointment. We had read " Eöthen," and had placed Mr. Kinglake amongst our literary gods. And when he was first pointed out to us we turned eagerly to look at the man who had so suddenly risen to fame on the strength of one small volume of travels, but, as we have said, we were disappointed, and though we have seen him often since we have not been called upon to correct our first impressions. Mr. Kinglake is an uncommon-looking man, but after repeated observations we see no indications of his power. But it must be remembered that we have only seen Mr. Kinglake in the lobby and in the House—in the lobby, which is so large and massive that it dwarfs and makes everybody look mean; and in the House, at a distance which precludes close observation, and where the light is so arranged as to distort the features of the members when they have their hats off, and to throw their faces into shade when they sit covered. Perhaps in a smaller chamber our impression of Mr. Kinglake's appearance might be corrected. Mr. Kinglake's advent into the House excited considerable expectations in the literary world, but it is not too much to say that they have hitherto been disappointed. Mr. Kinglake's first speech was almost a break-down. At every successive attempt, though he increased in confidence, he failed to command the House. And in his last display, that terribly long speech on the *Charles-et-Georges* affair—the dispute between France and Portugal about the French vessel alleged to be carrying slaves—when he spoke for two hours and a half, he so completely wearied the House that we fear we must reluctantly come to the decision that this brilliant writer is another parliamentary failure. We have always thought that our literary men do not consult their fame when they aspire to the House of Commons. It is ten to one against their succeeding, and if they fail, how is their fame damaged, and how does the nimbus of glory with which popular fancy surrounds them become dimmed! Let them, like the gods of old, speak to us from behind a cloud. They always become vulgarised and lose their power when they descend into the arena of worldly strife.

CHAPTER XI.

[In the Session of 1859 Lord Derby and Mr. Disraeli
introduced a Reform Bill, which proved to be a total failure.]

April 2, 1859. WHEN the Colonial Secretary rose to deliver
his views on the subject of Reform we knew
we might anticipate one of his " great orations." We all
know here when Sir Edward is going to speak as well as
we know that the sun is about to rise when a streak of
light appears over the eastern hills, or that it is going to
rain when thick, heavy clouds slowly roll up from the
south-west. When Sir Edward has made up his mind to
speak he is restless, uneasy, and wanders about the House
and the lobby with his hands in his pockets and his eyes
upon the ground. The Right Honourable Baronet has
lately made some change in the appearance of his outward
man. He used, until he took office, to wear a formidable
moustache and a long ragged " imperial," but he has now
clipped and trimmed these hirsute ornaments, and looks
neater and more like an Englishman than he did last year.
Sir Edward's speech is said to have been a grand oration.

Nay, one enthusiastic member declared that it was "one of the grandest orations which have ever been delivered in the House of Commons." To this, of course, we should demur, though we are not competent fully to decide upon its merits; for, in truth, though we listened attentively, we could not catch more than half of what the Right Honourable Baronet said. The voice we heard, but, alas, before it reached us it was only a voice; the articulate sounds, by the manner in which they were projected from the mouth, were, before they reached us, most of them inarticulate— mere sounds, conveying no meaning. On looking over Sir Edward's speech as reported in the *Times*, we find the following passage, than which few things finer have been uttered in the course of the debate: "The popular voice is like the grave; it cries 'give, give,' but like the grave, it never returns what it receives." Well, the condition in which this remark came up to us was something like this— "The popular yah! is like the grah! it cried yah! yah! but like the grah! it never returns." At the close of the sentence Sir Edward dropped his head so low that the last word or two went under the table. Members down below, we apprehend, must have heard Sir Edward better, for they cheered vociferously. Indeed, at the close of this remarkable harangue, the cheering was beyond everything that we ever heard in the House or indeed elsewhere. It was literally a "tempest of applause," and seemed to us to come from all parts of the House. It burst forth as the orator sat down like a hurricane, was renewed, and re-renewed, and then, when it seemed to have died out, was started again, and once more the whole House appeared to join in chorus. And all this was rendered more effective by the members rising just then to go to dinner, and cheering as they rose. A proud man was Sir Edward that night as members came up to congratulate him on his success, and

probably he went home and dreamed, either waking or
sleeping, that he had secured a great parliamentary name,
and that future historians will say of him that, in addition
to being a most successful novelist, he was one of the
greatest orators of his time.   Well, perhaps they may, and
with truth; but that, to our mind, is not saying much.   It
is only saying that he is one of the " Tritons of the
minnows," for every " great debate " which we hear only
still further confirms the opinion which we have often
uttered in these columns, that though we have many
eloquent and effective speakers we have no great orators.
As a test, let us ask ourselves the question—Will any one,
centuries hence, study the speeches delivered in this great
debate as scholars now study the orations of Demosthenes
and Cicero, or will our immediate descendants read them
with interest as we do the speeches of Burke, Erskine, or
Brougham?   We read them now because we are mixed up
in the political contest which rages, but ten years hence shall
we read them? and in 1959 will our descendants turn to
them as studies?

   But we must pass on—for all this while we have left an
Honourable Member waiting.   When Sir Edward sat down,
and whilst the storm was raging, and members were
everywhere on the wing, Mr. Byng arose, and was fortunate
enough to catch the Speaker's eye; but for several minutes
it was impossible for him to attempt to speak, for no voice—
not that of Stentor himself—could have lifted itself up above
the roar of that hurricane, and Mr. Byng's small voice
would have been no more than the piping of a wren in
a West Indian tornado.   And so Mr. Byng quietly waited
until the applause subsided, and the hungry crowd was
gone, and then began.   And what a contrast was the whole
scene to that which had just passed away!   Just now
the House was crammed, and there stood at the table a

fierce-looking man, vociferating and gesticulating as if he were mad, and the House every now and then broke out into a roar, as if the speaker had infected his hearers with his madness. Now the House is nearly empty—still and calm as a summer's eve, and, instead of the wild gesticulator, who had so lately lashed his audience to fury, there stands a pale, thin, diminutive youth, delivering a neat and polished and evidently well-studied address, in soft and musical tones, but with no more energy nor action than a young lady displays when she says her "poetry" to her governess. After a storm a calm is pleasant, but this is too calm—it is oppressive, or rather let us say soothing, lulling—for so we found it. For a time we resolutely listened, and for a time the gentle words came full upon our ears, and entered into the mind, but soon they became broken words, then they resolved into a mere humming, and at last the humming ceased altogether, and House and all its members passed away, and we dropped off into a profound, and—after the excitement of listening to and staring at the Colonial Secretary—a grateful slumber. How long we slept we cannot tell, but we were suddenly aroused by what appeared to us a terrific crash. At first we thought we were in our easy-chair at home, and that a tea-tray had been sacrificed; but soon the whole scene came full before us—the carved galleries, the yellow light, the gorgeous velvet curtains, and we found that it was not a crash but a cheer that broke our slumbers—a cheer to greet Mr. Sidney Herbert, who was now upon his legs. Mr. Sidney Herbert is what is called "a Peelite," but the term is fast going out of use. When parties changed sides in 1857 the Right Honourable Gentleman for a time flitted about the House, and had no settled seat. Sometimes he would drop into his old place, near Sir James Graham and Mr. Gladstone, on the Ministerial side below the gangway; then you might see him lower down, on the extreme right; but at length he quietly dropped down on the opposite side of the House, near Lord John Russell and Mr. Roebuck. Mr. Herbert is a tall, handsome, aristocratic-looking gentleman, with a fine face, and remarkably large, penetrating eyes. When he began to speak the House filled rapidly, for two reasons. First, he is an attractive speaker—delivers what he has to say in flowing, forcible language, accompanied by graceful action and bearing; and, secondly, as he occupies a somewhat singular position, not being pledged to either party, everybody was anxious to learn how he would pronounce on this great occasion. Mr. Herbert did not leave the House long in doubt, for, amidst the cheers of the Opposition, he at once opened fire against the Bill and its promoters, and in strong racy English analysed the measure, and turned the position of the Government inside out. Some of his taunts were very effective, and were received with great glee by the Opposition. "If we had shut our eyes," he said, "it would have been difficult to imagine that some of the orations which have been delivered from the Ministerial side of the House had not been spoken from this side." And again—"I don't go the length of some of my Conservative friends. I am not prepared for electoral districts." But we must leave Mr. Sidney Herbert. Perhaps when we have to notice him again in these columns he will be on the Ministerial Bench. He seems to be trending that way.

But we must hasten on to overtake the events of this busy week. On Thursday the principal performers were Mr. Bernal Osborne and Mr. Bright. The former arose about ten o'clock. It was suspected that Mr. Osborne meant to speak, and members were on the watch for his rising; and when it was reported in the lobbies and smokery that "Osborne was up," the knots of gossipers

and loungers were broken up, cigars were dropped, and
every man rushed into the House to see and hear and
enjoy the expected fun. And at the clubs, too, all was hurry-
scurry. For when Mr. Osborne arose the telegraph flashed
the news to Pall Mall; dinner-parties were broken up, and
in a minute every available cab was on the move. Mr.
Osborne's speech was pronounced to be a "great success."
It did not probably change an opinion, and certainly did not
gain a vote, but it kept the House in a roar of laughter and
cheers for an hour, and therefore was a success. We have
often been asked by persons who read, but have never
heard, Mr. Osborne's speeches, what there is in them that
so excites the House, and we confess that we could never
give a satisfactory answer. We have heard Mr. Osborne
often, and have joined in the merriment that he excited,
but when all was over we acknowledge that we could never
tell why we laughed; and reading the speech which excited
our mirth, we have not unfrequently had a feeling that
we had overnight played the fool. It is probably the
Honourable Member's manner more than his matter that
excites us. There is nothing particularly provocative of
sorrow in the word "Mesopotamia," but we are told that
Whitefield could make his audience weep by his manner of
pronouncing it. We think, however, that there can be no
doubt that the House of Commons is, of all assemblies that
we know, most easily excited to merriment. A foreign
friend of ours, who had visited the House, noticed this
peculiarity, and quietly remarked when he came home,
that he thought "the House of Commons was a most
laffable House."

After an interval of two hours, which were occupied by
Mr. Walpole, Mr. Bright arose. Mr. Walpole was listened
to with grave attention, for he stands in a peculiar position
just now; and, moreover, he is held in great respect by the

House—in greater respect now than ever, for it is felt that in throwing up his office, just at the time when he might have reasonably expected a handsome pension for life, he has made no small sacrifice for conscience' sake—but he could hardly keep the House together. One by one the members sidled out, and when he closed the House was visibly much thinner than when he began. But it filled again in a moment when Mr. Bright arose. In the division-lobbies, we were told, not a soul was to be seen. The library and smoking-room were deserted, and for an hour not a single member was observed to enter the House; but it was not the expectation of fun which now attracted the members, for in that sort of vanity Mr. Bright never indulges. He seldom laughs, does not even cheer, except on rare occasions, and never attempts to provoke merriment. Neither is it the characteristic of his speeches that they call forth cheers. The attention of the House, not its applause, is what the Member for Birmingham strives to obtain. And he succeeds—succeeds beyond any other speaker in the House. It is really a fine sight in the House when Bright is speaking. Every seat is occupied; crowds of men are standing at the bar and behind the chair; and in the side-galleries, which on ordinary occasions are vacant, the benches are all full. The reporters are all assiduously employed; and through the brass screen behind the ladies can be observed, eagerly listening to catch every word, those in the front rank flattening their faces against the network, and those behind stretching forward their heads over the shoulders of those in the front. This is the attitude in which we like best to see the House—an attitude of eager, rapt attention. And this is the attitude which we deem to be most flattering to the speaker. Not laughter, but attention, would please us best if we had to address the House; for we rather sympathise with that old orator who exclaimed, when the mirth of his audience was excited : " What foolish thing have I said that these people laugh ? " We have said that it is not the characteristic of Mr. Bright's speeches that they call forth cheers ; but it must not be thought that they are not cheered, for they are, and heartily too. Indeed, we fancy that no man's speeches are so *heartily* cheered—if the word " heartily " means " from the heart," as the dictionaries tell us it does. Of Mr. Bright's speech we can say nothing here, for our space fails, nor is there much occasion, as we have often spoken of the eloquence of this remarkable man.

The speech of the evening was Sir James Graham's, which was looked for with great anxiety, for though rumours were afloat that the " old Knight of Netherby " would oppose the Government, nothing was certain until the Right Honourable Baronet arose and pronounced. Now, however, the question is decided, for never was there delivered in the House of Commons a more crushing, damaging, " mischievous " speech than that which Sir James delivered against the Government Reform Bill on Monday night. It was a speech that no one in the world, besides Sir James, could have delivered. So " wickedly conceived," as a Government member said, so artfully contrived, so coldly, deliberately, and with such evident, mischievous purpose, was it uttered, that it made us, whilst we listened, almost pity those at whom it was aimed. Listening to this speech was like standing by in one of the torture chambers of the Inquisition, whilst some grim unfeeling executioner was slowly torturing a poor wretch upon the rack.

April 9, 1859. On Monday sen'night Mr. Gladstone moved the adjournment of the debate, and on the following day, in conformity with parliamentary usage, he

was called upon to re-open it. As it was known that Mr.
Gladstone would speak, the House was densely crowded in
every part. Every seat was occupied; every step was
turned into a seat. At the bar and behind the Speaker's
chair crowds of members clustered who could find no seats,
and in the side-galleries both the benches were closely
packed. Mr. Gladstone arose about 5.30, and it was evident
to every one that the Right Honourable Gentleman was in
capital feather. Generally Mr. Gladstone's face looks pale
and faded, but all this was gone. His eye was bright—the
ashy hue was changed to an olive brown, and even the
furrows on his careworn cheek seemed to be filled up. His
journey to the Isles of Greece—however otherwise unprofit-
able—has evidently improved the Right Hon. Gentleman's
health, appearance, and spirits. Just before he arose to
address the House there was a buzz of conversation and
much moving about and restlessness, as there always is
whilst the preliminary business of the evening is going on;
but when Mr. Speaker called out " Mr. Gladstone " the
conversation died away, the confusion resolved itself into
order, and when the well-known form of " the great
Rhetorician " was seen to rise out of the crowd, and the
tones of his voice were heard, all noise was hushed down in
a moment to the deepest silence, and every eye was turned
towards the speaker. In the words of Milton,

> " —— His voice
> Drew audience and attention still as night,
> Or summer's noontide air."

The deep silence in the House suddenly produced by the
rising of one of its favourite speakers is always impressive,
and it was never more so than on this occasion. It
has been said that in proportion as men rise in culture,
eloquence must lose its power: but it is a foolish saying.

The same has been said of poetry, music, and the fine arts;
but experience, and fact, and philosophy every day refute
the theory. It is one of the eternal laws that mind can
influence mind. In common matters the medium of this
influence takes the form of plain prose; in high, of oratory;
in higher, of poetry; and in highest, when the thought is
unutterable in words, it bursts forth in music; or more
deliberately expresses itself in painting, sculpture, or even
architecture. There may be men who are insensible to
thought thus expressed, but that is not because they are
too highly, but because they are not sufficiently, cultured; or
it may be because they have a defective nature. But we
must not stop to philosophise.

Mr. Gladstone spoke for more than two hours, and he
never spoke with more vigour and fluency; but if we are
asked whether on this occasion his speech was effective—
whether it contained anything worth remembering? we fear
we must say no. And if, as Cicero says, " Oratory is
nothing else than wisdom speaking copiously," we fear that
we must decide that this is not oratory—for though the
copiousness was there, we failed to discern the wisdom.
There were words in profusion; fluency not to be matched
in the speeches of any other speaker; and there were
musical tones, correct elocution, and forcible, if not graceful action; but nothing wise, nothing great, nothing worth
remembering. As a specimen of Mr. Gladstone's copiousness, we just give the following paraphrases which he used
to describe mere nomination boroughs:—" They are small
boroughs, the constituencies of which, from kindly interests,
from ancient and affectionate recollection, from local and
traditional respect, from remembrance of services received,
from the admiration of great men and great qualities, are
willing to take upon trust the candidates recommended to
them *by those noblemen or gentlemen who stand in immediate*

connection with them." This is speaking copiously—but is it wisdom that speaks?

But we must now jump to the last night of the debate— that night big with the fall of more than a hundred men— for in consequence of the proceedings of that night it is next to certain that upwards of a hundred Members will soon disappear from the House and never be seen there again. It was Thursday, the last day of March, when this debate, which had lasted seven nights, came to a close—or rather Friday; for though the debate recommenced early on Thursday evening, it did not finish until Friday morning. During the early part of the evening there was some little doubt whether a division could take place. All the leaders were anxious for it, but there were still many members who wished to speak, if not to influence the debate, "to justify their votes to their constituents"; and probably some of these might insist upon a further adjournment. But during the dinner-hour most of these speeches to "bunkum" were worked off. At half-past ten Mr. Roebuck arose, and matters looked promising. And when he sat down and Mr. Disraeli got up, we all knew that the end was come.

Mr. Disraeli's speech was to our minds one of the greatest that he ever delivered. And yet we can easily imagine that strangers in the gallery were disappointed. Mr. Disraeli has a widespread reputation for brilliancy, wit, sarcasm, and invective, but there was little of all that on this occasion. The Right Honourable Gentleman was in quite a different position from that which he occupied when he hurled those fierce invectives against Sir Robert Peel, and he knew it. He was then the keen, reckless, unscrupulous assailant, but now he is himself on his defence. And from his tone, and manner, and bearing it was easy to see that (to use one of his favourite phrases) he felt in full force "the gravity of the occasion." His manner was calm and dignified, his voice was subdued and at times solemn, and instead of that brilliancy to which we have been accustomed, we had measured and stately phrases ; and in the place of sarcasm, and wit, and ingenious paradox we had argument and warning. And how changed, too, was his manner ! There are now none of the " tricks of the orator." He did not pull down his waistcoat, or thrust his hands into its pockets, or hook his fingers in its armholes. Indeed, as if he were conscious that these his accustomed attitudes and movements would be out of place, he had carefully buttoned his surtout closely across his chest before he began. Neither did he turn round to his followers to evoke their laughter and cheers, as he is wont ; but standing erect and for the most part, especially in the more serious parts of his speech, with arms folded tightly across his breast, he fixed his deep-seated but glittering eyes steadily upon his foes.

But though Disraeli was delivering certainly one of his greatest speeches, it is remarkable that the House was not nearly so full as it was when Gladstone spoke. The fact was that many of the Members were too excited, as the division approached, to sit quietly in the House, and so they wandered about the lobbies and the library, or tried to calm their nerves with a quiet smoke below. This comparative thinness of the House led to a good deal of speculation and doubt for a time. There were not more than 500 members present. " Where were the others ? " was anxiously asked. " Are they Conservatives or Oppositionists that are absent ? " The impression seemed to be that they were the latter, and for a time the Ministerial " whips " and their friends were in high glee. " Our men are all here ; their men won't come to the scratch, you'll see ; we shall beat them like a sack," we heard one of the Government Members say. But soon Disraeli dropped into his seat, the Speaker arose to put the question, the division-bell rang, and then we saw another sight; for members now poured inward in shoals, and most of those who came up were evidently not "our men." And as the stream rolled on the hopes of the Conservatives were damped, and their hearts failed them. But see, the door is shut, and all are in at last; and soon all doubt and speculation will be over. The excitement in the lobby whilst the division was on was intense; not a few Peers were there; election agents on the *qui vive* for a dissolution; and friends and partisans of the Government and of their opponents in large numbers. And as the five-and-twenty minutes which the division occupied slowly wore away the suspense was painful. But listen, there is some news; what did that member say through the grating on the door—"Ayes 291? Why, there must surely be a majority, for there cannot be 600 in the House." And for a . time the hopes of the Conservatives in the lobby, and of many inside, were in the ascendant. And well they might be—for to the uninitiated it might very well appear that 291 must win; but it did not appear so to us—who are not uninitiated—and for the following reasons: first, we strongly suspected, from what we had observed with our practised eye, that there were more than 600 members inside; and, secondly, we reckoned that if the "Ayes" had all gone in, and the "Noes" were still entering, the probability was that the "Noes" were most numerous. However, we were not much longer in suspense, for some uproarious cheering was heard. Another message came out, that the Government was beaten, for the Opposition tellers were on the right; and in another minute the door burst open, and a dozen voices shouted out: "Majority against the Government, 39."

The confusion and excitement and noise in the lobby on the announcement of the numbers are things which cannot be described; you might as well try to photograph a cloud of fireflies. There were hurryings hither, hurryings thither. Messengers, who had previously secured hansom cabs, were scudding away with the numbers to all parts of the metropolis. Members were rushing to the telegraph office to flash the news to their friends in the country; the "whips" were busy in keeping their forces together in expectation of another division—but we must leave this scene to the imagination, and pass on to show what was going on in the House. And first let us briefly explain to our readers the state of the question after the division. The original question was "that the bill be read a second time." The amendment of Lord John was that "all the words after the word 'that' be left out, in order to insert" his proposition, which we need not give. The question, then, which the Speaker had just put was, "That the words proposed to be left out (viz., all the words after 'that') stand part of the question." This had been negatived, and therefore the only word left in the original question was, "*that*." The next question to be put was that Lord John Russell's amendment be added after the word "that"; and it was on this question that it was thought that another division might take place. No division, however, did take place. Some zealous Conservatives wished for one, but Mr. Disraeli gave no encouragement to the move, and so Lord John's amendment was added *nem. con.*

If a bombshell had fallen amongst the members on Monday night they could not have been more startled than they were by the announcement made by Mr. Disraeli that Parliament is to be dissolved. It is true that rumour had been rife for weeks that it would come to this. And the *Morning Star* had announced in the morning that this was the decision of the Government, but still very few believed it; and when, after long and torturing preliminary descriptions of what the Government might have done—or would have done if that had occurred which didn't occur—or that had not happened which did happen—Mr. Disraeli uttered the fatal word, it was easy to see that a large number of the members had got what they didn't bargain for when they divided against the Government last week. But the words had been uttered and could not be recalled. All must go and meet their constituents. Many must incur expenses which they can ill afford; and not a few, at least one-third of the whole, will never come back. For an hour there was quite a crowd of members at the telegraph office that night. Many were busy penning their election addresses, whilst not a few posted off to catch the train, and proceed at once to solicit the sweet voices of their constituents. In about sixteen days from this time Parliament will be dissolved; and in five weeks, or thereabout, it will once more assemble.

April 23, 1859. To the last it was uncertain whether the House would be prorogued on Tuesday; and nothing was actually known until the doorkeeper shouted in the lobby, "Half-past one to-morrow." Then we all knew that the thing was settled—for the House never meets at that hour excepting to be prorogued. And now all is over. The House assembled at the time appointed. There was no need for the presence of forty members — for "the commission makes a House" — *i.e.*, whenever there is a commission from the Crown the House is considered "made," although not a member may be present. About two, Black Rod knocked at the door for admission to summon the House to the Peers, and having delivered his message, Mr. Speaker, preceded by the mace, marched away, followed by some score of members, and, as far as we here were concerned, all was over. The Parliament of 1857 had vanished. It still exists in law, and will exist till the dissolution appears in the *Gazette;* but it will never appear in the House again.

CHAPTER XII.

REAPPEARANCE OF RICHARD COBDEN—A SPIRITED DEBATE —"SAM SLICK."

July 9, 1859. RICHARD COBDEN has once more made his appearance in the House. He landed at Liverpool on the 29th ult., and on the following Friday he came to the House and took the oaths and his seat. Very cordial were the greetings which awaited Mr. Cobden in the lobby, and as he marched up to the table a hearty cheer testified to the general joy which was felt that the great apostle of free trade was once more in his right place. It was in 1841 that Mr. Cobden first became a member of Parliament, and Stockport had the honour of sending him there. At the general election in 1847 he was elected for both Stockport and the West Riding, and, of course, chose to sit for the latter. In 1857 he retired, however, from Yorkshire, and offered Huddersfield the honour of returning him to the House; but just then a fit of madness had come over the constituencies, and Huddersfield refused the honour, and sent instead Mr. Akroyd, the great worsted manufacturer, and Mr. Cobden went to America. The journey to the United States, we have reason to believe, was undertaken to settle private business there, and had no political object; and it was Mr. Cobden's wish quietly to transact his business and then return. But it is very diffi-

cult for kings to travel *incog*. Mr. Cobden's fame had preceded him. He found that he was almost as well known
there as he is in his own country; and, though he shunned
public receptions, he could not escape recognition, and
everywhere he was recognised and received the most marked
respect. Railway companies, it is said, insisted upon his
travelling free, and in some cases the hotelkeepers refused
to take his money. We are happy to be able to report that
Mr. Cobden looks well after his voyage. When we last saw
him he looked haggard and distressed; and no wonder, for
then he had just lost his only son. The promising youth
was at school in Germany, where he was taken suddenly ill,
and before his parents could receive the intelligence of his
illness he was dead. It was an awful blow—so staggering
that for a time we feared that we never should see Cobden
in the House again. But, as one says, "the heart of man
is strong in asserting its right to joy"; and Mr. Cobden was
too wise a man to oppose its assertion of this right. And
now here he is again, once more, to do honour to the English
Parliament. Mr. Cobden, though, won't take office, and
herein he is right. What lustre can office add to the name
of Richard Cobden that would compensate for the loss of the
freedom which he now breathes and feels? Mr. Cobden's
mission is not to rule, but to teach—to teach great political
truths. In "the good time coming" there may possibly be
a place for men of Cobden's school, but there is, we venture
to say, none now. Meanwhile let us be consoled by reflect-
ing that, next to an able Government, it is important that
we have an able Opposition.

July 30, 1859. In the House of Commons we never know
what a night may bring forth. We go down
sometimes expecting a long and interesting debate, when lo!
the motion is suddenly withdrawn; and, instead of sitting

until after midnight, we are up and away by seven. At other times the "order paper" looks so innocent that we say "There is nothing here to keep us," and we indulge in a hope that we shall speedily be dismissed; but suddenly some speaker arises, introduces a new and disputable topic, and at the moment when we are dreaming of a quiet stroll in the park, or a visit to the Opera, or of dropping in upon a friend just as he is sitting down to dinner, we discover that we are in for a long discussion and a late night. Everything is uncertain in the world, but nothing is so uncertain, surely, as the proceedings of the English House of Commons. On Thursday, the 21st, for example, the programme of the evening seemed simple enough. The first "order" was "Ways and Means," to enable Mr. Gladstone to move in Committee his financial resolutions; the second was "Supply"; and, as no intimation had been whispered that the "resolutions" were to be opposed, it was expected that they would pass *sub silentio*, and that then we should get into "Supply," and have a long, dull night at the "Miscellaneous Estimates." But, on throwing a glance of our experienced eye over the House at five o'clock, we were at once led to suspect that something would turn up to disappoint our expectations. The Ministerial bench was full. On the Opposition side all the ex-Ministers had mustered, and below the gangway, on the Government side of the House, sat Bright and Cobden, and, further, Bright had an ominous-looking paper in his hand, which appeared very much like notes of a speech, and soon our suspicions were confirmed, for when the clerk had called out the first order—"Ways and Means," and Mr. Gladstone had taken off his hat, and muttered "that Mr. Speaker do leave the chair," Mr. Disraeli arose, and by the manner of his rising, and by the tone of the first sentence of his exordium, we knew that he meant to do battle.

Every one knows on his rising when Mr. Disraeli means to make a long speech. When he only intends to offer a few interlocutory remarks he leans over the table, speaks in a low tone to the gentlemen opposite, and shows by his manner of standing and speaking that he intends soon to sit down. But when he arises for an oration he starts bolt upright at once, lays his notes on the official box before him, steps a pace backwards, pulls down his waistcoat, brings his arms into position, and waits until due silence is secured. Mr. Disraeli's office on this occasion was to defend his financial operation, and in some degree the foreign policy of the late Government. When the right honourable gentleman delivered his financial statement in 1858 he made all things fair and square upon paper. He estimated the revenue in round numbers at £64,000,000, the actual receipts were £65,500,000; and yet when he left office there was a deficiency of about £5,000,000, and he naturally enough wished to show to the country how this occurred, and we venture to say that he did this with complete success. The estimate of the revenue, so far from being too sanguine, had been exceeded, and his estimate of the expenditure would have been correct but for the disturbing influence of the war, and the consequent necessity for a large increase in the army and navy expenditure. This first part of Mr. Disraeli's speech, though able and successful, was of course somewhat dull, for who can be eloquent in dealing with figures? The House, however, listened with due gravity, and, on the whole, was satisfied, though it was not excited to cheers; but when he came to the latter part of his speech, in which he touched upon foreign policy, he was all himself again, brought down loud cheers from his party, and applause from many of his opponents, and managed to touch a chord, when he advised a closer amity with France, that we may reduce our armaments, and thus terminate "this disastrous and wild expenditure," that did not cease to vibrate during the whole of the debate.

But the most noticeable feature in Mr. Disraeli's speech was the fine vein of ironic sarcasm which ran through the latter part. Mr. Disraeli is nothing unless he be sarcastic. Sometimes his sarcasm is blunt and somewhat coarse, but here it was as fine and delicate as a razor's edge. The late Government had been taunted with being the friends of Austria, and with having no sympathy or friendship with France. "We have been told," said he, "that it was entirely from the absence of some of those distinguished statesmen from the bench opposite which they now so pre-eminently adorn (!) that the war broke out at all. Had they been there it is well known that the Emperor of the French would never have taken a single step without consulting them," &c., &c. And then he went on to intimate that now they were in power they had a fine opportunity to exercise their influence, and he exhorted them earnestly to exert it to induce the Emperor to reduce his armaments, that we may reduce ours. The Opposition saw, appreciated, and cheered lustily this irony, and it seemed also to take the fancy of the gentlemen below the gangway on the other side, for they also joined in the cheers.

We were curious to observe closely Mr. Disraeli's countenance when he was thus speaking, to see if there were there any signs of feeling, but we saw, as usual, none. Mr. Disraeli's face, to those who are at some distance, and in most cases even to those who are near him, is simply the most unimpassioned countenance that ever stood upon the shoulders of a man. At a distance you can see no more expression than you would upon the face of an automaton, it is so utterly emotionless and inexpressive. In his deep-set eyes not a twinkle is discernible, nor is there the slightest movement about the lips, excepting that which is necessary

to expel the words. When you are close to him you may
occasionally fancy that you discern a faint radiance in his
eyes; and when his sarcasm is more than uncommonly biting
there is a slight sardonic movement in the upper lip; but
these signs are at no time more than faintly discernible. It
is not a nice countenance to contemplate. It is not English,
open, attractive. We could never fancy children being
attracted by it. The face of a man ought to be—and would
always be if he would let it—the index of the nature within.
It should light up when he is joyful, flash when he is angry,
plainly speak of sorrow when he is in distress, and writhe
when he is in pain. Nature intended it to do all this; but
it may be said that nature has, probably, denied to Mr.
Disraeli this power. We don't believe it. Thirty years ago,
when Mr. Disraeli stood upon the hustings at Wycombe, as
a " young and curly " aspirant to Parliamentary honours, we
may rely upon it his face was not the dull and passionless
surface that it is now. Young, ardent, passionate, and
hopeful, he let it show what he felt, and permitted it, by its
varied expression, to give force to his fervid words. But a
long course of official caution and reserve has hardened his
features and destroyed their natural flexibility. To keep the
muscles of our body flexible we must use them; by dis-
continuing to use them we lose their power.

Very different was the appearance of the Chancellor of the
Exchequer when he leaped from his seat to reply to his predecessor. He was evidently excited; and in countenance,
manner, and bearing he showed his excitement. Mr. Bright,
by watching his opportunity, succeeded in getting first upon
his legs, and must "have caught the eye of the Speaker "
first. But this phrase has a technical meaning when it is
said that " Mr. So-and-so first caught the Speaker's eye." It
is not understood that it was literally so, but rather that Mr.
So-and-so was the man whom the Speaker wished to address

the House. Generally, the first that rises gets precedence, but when a Cabinet Minister rises Mr. Speaker calls upon him in preference to any other. There were loud cries, and long continued, for Mr. Bright, and for a time Mr. Bright stood his ground. But Mr. Gladstone, in a somewhat defiant manner, kept his position. He had been called upon by the Speaker, and he maintained his right against all claimants, and soon the clamour weakened, and at length died away. It has been noticeable that Mr. Gladstone has spoken with more energy and excitement since he has been in office; and, being more excited, he has been more concise and less diffuse. On the subject of the Roman Catholic claims he broke forth, in answer to a speech from Mr. Whiteside, like a tornado; and, though he spoke for not more than twenty minutes, he compressed into his speech such forcible arguments, such pregnant facts, and such withering sarcasm, that he made the Attorney-General for Ireland writhe in his seat. And, on opening his Budget, it was a subject of general remark how closely the Chancellor stuck to his subject, and how plain, and lucid, and concise he was in his statements. We know not that we ever listened to a more masterly statement. On former similar occasions Mr. Gladstone has spoken for four hours and more, but on this he only occupied two, and on the occasion in question he was equally forcible and concise. Some of his sentences were epigrammatic in their terseness. But the speech of the evening was that delivered by Mr. Bright.

It was known to Mr. Bright's friends that he had a speech on the anvil, and it was expected that it would be a great one, though we know not whether it was understood that he would launch it that night. We have read the speech in the morning papers. The *Times* reports it best, but only a faint idea can be formed from reading of the force and power with which it was delivered, and of its effect upon the House.

But, nevertheless, we, who have often heard Mr. Bright, and have reflected carefully upon his speaking, have come to the conclusion that Mr. Bright owes more of his power in the House to his matter than to his manner. He is a capital speaker, no doubt. His action is simple and unaffected; his voice is good; his language is pure and forcible, but his greatest power in the House lies not there. In the House of Commons there is a conventional mode of treating all subjects which come before it. Very few speakers seem to us to speak *ex animo*. Few of them seem to tread firmly, as if they felt the solid earth under them, but delicately, timidly, and apologetically, as if they were afraid of offending against some established conventionalism or shocking some prejudice. But when Mr. Bright arises, and after you have listened to a few sentences, you feel that you have a manly Englishman before you, one who believes earnestly that he has got something to say and is determined to say it, let him who will be offended or him who will be pleased. He is a Martin Luther-like man, who would go to Worms " were all the tiles on the houses devils." He never goes about a subject and about it, but shears through every intervening obstacle of pre-judice, and conventionalism, and etiquette, right to the heart of the matter at once. Take his speech on the occasion in question; read it carefully, and you will at once see what he means. " Oh, yes, you must have the income tax, I know; you cannot do without it; but it is an odious tax. And why is it odious? Because it is a tax upon property? No; but because it is unjustly levied. You farmers, for instance, why should not you pay as much on your incomes as others do on theirs? And then there's the succession duty, can anything be more unjust than that? There was a gentleman lately who had a landed estate, worth £32,000, left him by a person who was no relative. Now, if this had been left in money the duty would have been £3,200, but being a landed estate the duty was only £700. Is that just? Is it consistent with fairness?—is it consistent with our personal honour?—for, after all, that comes into the question—is it consistent with our duty to society that we should take the class of property the most select, attracting towards it many social and practical advantages, having in it the most certain means of accumulation and improvement?—is it fair, I say, that we should take this property and charge it only £700; whilst on another description of property, that is not worth a bit more in the market, we should charge £3,200?" Now, this is going to the heart of the matter; and this is a fair specimen of the manner in which Mr. Bright treats all subjects which come before him in the House. As he and Mr. Cobden did in the Corn-law war, so he does now—dashing through all the outworks right up to the citadel, and demanding its surrender. Our space is running short, but we must just notice the peroration of this remarkable speech, and we are more anxious to do so because in several papers it is wrongly given:—"I pray," said the hon. gentleman, "that there may soon come a time when the Government of this country may take such steps as I have indicated for the bringing about a state of things between France and England which shall unite these two great nations in a bond of permanent amity, and show that eighteen hundred years of the *profession* of Christian doctrine is at length to be *compensated* by something like Christian practice." In a report which lies before me the word profession is left out, and for " compensated " the reporter has written " consummated," by which change a neat little bit of satire is wholly spoiled. The hon. gentleman, we need hardly say, resumed his seat amidst a storm of cheers. After him came Lord John, who, however, spoke but little; and Lord Palmerston, who spoke long, but with not much effect. Indeed, the noble Lord's speaking days are passed. Every one must have noticed a change in his

Lordship this Session : that slow but sure sleuth-hound, old age, has got him in wind at last, if not in grasp.

On Monday last Mr. Judge Haliburton ("Sam Slick") made his maiden speech.   When he arose the House was hushed to silence in a moment, but his speech was not a success, and it is clear now that Mr. Haliburton, racy writer as he is, is no orator.   The characteristic of Mr. Haliburton's works is rollicking fun and humour, but there was nothing of this sort in his speech.   It was just such a speech as any country gentleman might have made.   The appearance of Mr. Haliburton is that of a sturdy old gentleman farmer, utterly unlike what from reading his works you would imagine him to be.   He is, according to Dod, only sixty-three years old, but he looks older.   We should from his appearance take him to be at least seventy.

CHAPTER XIII.

NOTABLES—MR. GLADSTONE'S BUDGET.

Aug. 6, 1859. WE have often said that the lobby of the House of Commons is the place of all others in the world where the great notables of the time may be seen. There is scarcely a man of high political character in Europe whom we have not seen there. Count Cavour used occasionally to flit across to his place in the Ambassadors' gallery ; the Marquis d'Azeglio was, at one time, a constant attendant on the debates ; Mr. Buchanan, the President of the United States, while he was Minister here, was seldom absent when a great discussion was on; the Count de Montalembert, as his celebrated work shows, was a frequent visitor to the House of Commons : indeed, time and space would fail if we were to attempt to enumerate the great men who have passed across this busy scene. Some week or two ago M. de Persigny might be seen lounging against one of the pedestals. He was waiting for Lord Palmerston, with whom he had a long interview in a neighbouring room. If we recollect rightly it was on the day when the telegraphic wires had flashed suddenly the unexpected news that there was again peace in Italy. Unfortunately we have but an indistinct remembrance of most of these men. They appear, we hear their names, they flit across the stage like phantasmagoria. They are

here—they are gone. Some of them we recollect well, whilst
others are mere shadows.   Buchanan has left a distinct
image on our minds : he is tall, bulky, and not prepossessing
in his appearance, and has, if we mistake not, something of
a cross in his eye.   Montalembert's face is well known to
the British public, as portraits of the illustrious politician
and eloquent writer are not uncommon.   We miss, however,
in almost all of them the thoughtfulness which we discerned
in the countenance of this famous man.   Persigny is short,
and not imposing in his appearance.

On the night when Lord John Russell delivered his statement on foreign affairs the lobby was crowded, and many
English notables were present ; but of foreign celebrities we
saw but few.   The man who most attracted our attention
was Sir John Lawrence.   We have seldom seen a more
striking-looking man than Sir John : he is in appearance the
very beau-ideal of a commander of men.   He is tall, but not
too tall—about five feet ten inches we take to be his height.
Your great man is seldom overgrown.   Very few of the
great men of history have exceeded this height.   Giants in
bulk are myths of a barbarous age.   Sir John's frame is
squarely built, and closely knit, with nothing like corpulent
development.   His forehead is good, but not remarkable ; his
features are strongly marked, but there are no indications of
anxiety and earthly cares ; they are rather the features of a
man who has had to contend with great difficulties, but who
has also had resolution and energy to confront and overcome
them.   The eye is dark and penetrating ; his cheekbones are
prominent, but not too high ; his lips are compressed, and
his upper lip is long and firm, showing that he can be sternly
resolute when required.   On the whole, we have seldom
seen a man whose whole appearance gives us so strongly
the idea of wisdom and power.   In the council-chamber or
the field we should judge that Sir John would be equally at

home.   The well-known description of Marmion came into
our minds involuntarily when Sir John stood before us—

> " His square-turned joints and strength of limb
> Showed him no carpet knight so trim,
> But in close fight a champion grim,
>   In camp a leader sage."

Sir John is not a soldier by profession, we know; but he has
shown, in more instances than one, that had he been trained
to arms he would have been as great a General as he is known
to be a wise and energetic Governor.

Very different in appearance is Sir James Brooke, whom
we saw wandering in the lobby with a friend the other day.
When we remembered what the hero of Sarawak has done,
we were disappointed with the appearance of Sir James.
But he is evidently worn down by fatigue and the anxieties
and cares which he has undergone, and looks as if he were
suffering, or just recovering, from a wasting fever.   Still,
there never could have been anything very remarkable in his
personal presence.   He is just an average-looking man,
nothing more.   Nature generally stamps her favourites with
an unmistakable mark, but not always.   Sometimes, in a
freakish mood, she refuses to give us any of the outward and
visible signs of the inward power.   Sir James Brooke, for
instance, though of common appearance, is a long way from
being a common man.

We have another instance of the waywardness of Nature
in this respect in a nobleman of no mean celebrity, who is
not infrequently now in the lobby—to wit, Lord Stratford
de Redcliffe, better known in diplomacy as Sir Stratford
Canning.   This remarkable man has been connected with
the diplomatic service for half a century, during which time
he has represented his country at almost every Court in
Europe, and once went across the Atlantic on a special
mission to Washington.   But it was reserved for Constanti-

nople to be the scene of his most eminent services.   He was
our Ambassador at the Court of the Sultan in 1841, and did
not permanently abdicate his high position until 1857 ; and
such was his influence and power there that he was generally
considered to be a sort of Viceroy.   Indeed, sometimes it
appeared as though the Sultan was King, and his Lordship
" Viceroy over him."   Perhaps it would be wrong to call Lord
Stratford de Redcliffe a great man ; but that he has shown
himself to be something more than common there cannot be
a doubt.   Yet, as we have hinted, there are few or no indications of power in his appearance.   And, as the little grey-
headed, pale-faced old gentleman glides across the lobby, you
would never single him out as anybody remarkable.   Perhaps, on a closer view than is permitted to vulgar people like
ourselves, indications might be discernible of power, but from
the distance at which we have been placed we could discern
none.   Report says that he is a most able administrator, and
perhaps he is so ; but, if this be the case, Nature has in this
instance waywardly neglected to authenticate her work with
her usual stamp.   As Lord Stratford de Redcliffe works his
sinuous way through the crowd in the lobby, or as he sits in
his place in the House of Peers, we should never deem him
to be more than a cunning diplomatist, and not even that if
we had not known his history.

But see, here is a great man and no mistake !   That is the
world-renowned Lord Brougham and Vaux.   He is not going
to the Commons, we will venture to say, for that he never
does.   No ; you see him turn the other way.   What a
queer-looking figure it is !   See how loosely his clothes hang
about him.   That hat of his, too, how closely it is pulled
over his brow !   It is not, however, a whim of his to wear it
so, but necessity compels him, for his forehead is so large
that he could never keep his hat on unless he were to draw
it well over his brow.   He looks very, very old now, and well

he may, for he is in or over his eighty-first year. For such
an age he walks well; and see how volubly he is chatting to
the friend on whose arm he hangs. It would be worth something now to know what he is talking about :—perhaps our
foreign relations, or it may be the last discovered fossilised
fish, or the Palace of the People at Muswell Hill, or some
new machine, or fresh theory of light; or—but it is in vain
to conjecture, for what subject is there that can come amiss
to Henry Brougham? His head is a perfect museum, and,
perhaps, it would be easier to say what he cannot talk about
than what he can. There is a joke abroad that one day at a
conversazione he was talking learnedly about a Hindoo poem
written 500 years B.C., when suddenly, on some hint given,
he began to discourse with equal knowledge on the philosophy
of cooking a beefsteak.

At a morning sitting, last week, an accident happened
which very much annoyed sundry honourable members.
The case was this:—During a morning sitting members
are very erratic, will not stop in the House to hear the
debate, but wander about the building—some into the
library, others to lunch in the dining-room, not a few to
smoke on the river terrace, whilst others lounge in the committee-rooms to watch the proceedings there, trusting to the
bells to recall them to the House when a division is announced.
Now, on the morning in question there was more than the
usual number in the committee-rooms upstairs, and not a
few in No. 1, at the further end of the gallery. About three
o'clock a division was called, and from all quarters of the
building a host of wanderers rushed into the House; but
somehow it happened that the batch in No. 1 did not hear
the bell in the corridor, or else the bell was out of order and
didn't ring—authorities differ on this point—and the consequence was that the said members did not start until some
time after the division had been called. It appears, however,

that they accidentally heard that the division was on, and then rushed out helter-skelter to be present; but, alas! when they arrived the door was shut. Loud were the complaints that they had been disappointed. And it was a mortifying occurrence, for this was the church-rate division, in which it was highly important that their names should appear. But there was no remedy; the door was shut, and when once closed it is never opened until the division ends. It is an exciting scene in a committee-room when a division is called. The chairman is in his chair, flanked on each side by his fellow-members, all listening to the eloquent harangue of Mr. Serjeant Buzfuz, when suddenly the tinkle of a bell is heard, and in a moment, without the slightest ceremony, up jump the chairman and committee and listening members, and away they rush, leaving Mr. Buzfuz with nothing before him but empty chairs and a blank wall.

Feb. 11, 1860. Monday was to have been a grand night. Most of the members were in town, and every seat set apart for strangers had long been taken. Almost every member had given his order for " the Strangers' Gallery." The lists for the Speaker's and ladies' galleries might have been filled a dozen times over, and no doubt the peers' and diplomatic seats would have been filled to crowding. This is not to be wondered at. Gladstone delivering his Budget alone would be sufficiently attractive to fill the House at any time; but this occasion was of peculiar interest, for, perhaps there has not been so important a Budget as this since the days of Sir Robert Peel. Rumours of all kinds flew about the lobby on Monday night touching the illness of the great Chancellor of the Exchequer. Some said he had diphtheria; others would have it that his disease was serious congestion of the lungs; whilst a few of the baser sort whispered about that he was not ill at all,. but, being unprepared, he was shamming to gain time.

We ourselves were accosted by one of these whisperers :
"This is a queer move, is it not?" said he. "What move?"
"Why, this move of Gladstone shamming illness." "Why,
you surely do not really believe that he is shamming?—why
shouldn't he be ill? Have Ministers of State immunities
from colds?" Whereupon our friend shrugged his shoulders,
looked at us out of the corner of his eye, and went his way
evidently astonished at our simplicity, and congratulating
himself on his own superior sagacity and penetration. Well,
thought we, go your ways—go your ways. You are cunning,
clever, sagacious, no doubt; but, rather than possess that
small, vulpine, suspicious intellect of yours we would consent
to be deceived every day of our lives.

Feb. 18, 1860. When the House opened on Thursday night
it was still somewhat doubtful whether Mr.
Gladstone would be strong enough for his work on Friday.
Late in the evening, however, a letter was received by Lord
Palmerston from Mrs. Gladstone, informing his Lordship
that her husband had received Dr. Ferguson's full permission
to return to the House on the following day. Thus the
question was set at rest. On Friday we need hardly say that
the anxiety to get into the House was general and intense.
[It had become well known that the Budget was to be
emphatically a Free Trade scheme, and to be founded, in
great measure, on the Commercial Treaty with France.]
There were "strangers" in attendance with orders as early
as eleven o'clock, and long before the House opened the
waiting-room was filled, and some forty or fifty people were
ranged in St. Stephen's Hall. Many of these, of course, did
not get in. They had members' orders; but orders, when
there is no room, are as useless as a cheque upon a bank
when there are "no effects." The Speaker's gallery was
crammed as soon as it was opened; and as to the Peers, they

came down in such numbers that, after the seats which are set apart for them were filled, they besieged the Ambassadors' gallery and filled up every available seat there, and even then many of them were obliged to stand in the passage at the back of the benches. Amongst the peers that were present we noticed particularly the venerable Lord Chancellor, Lord Stratford de Redcliffe; his Royal Highness the Duke of Cambridge, who commands our Forces; the First Lord of the Admiralty, the Duke of Somerset; his Grace the Duke of Argyll, who presides over our Post Office; Earl Granville, the Lord President of the Council; Earl Stanhope, Lord Stanley of Alderley, Earl De Grey and Ripon, Lord Chelmsford, Lord Wensleydale; the Earl of Derby, who for a time was obliged to stand; and last, though not least by a long way, Lord Brougham. The Foreign Ambassadors were not there in large numbers. Mr. Dallas was present, and two or three more, including Count Persigny; but the diplomatic body was not represented in such strength as it usually is on great occasions. Touching Lord Brougham we have to record a curious fact. The noble Lord left the Lower for the Upper House in 1832, twenty-eight years ago, and until that night had never honoured the scene of his former triumphs with his presence. Until Friday night he had never even seen the new House. Surely this is a strange fact. It would be interesting to know the reason why the noble Lord has never availed himself of his privilege of listening to the debates of that assembly in which he won his fame and honours. Lord Brougham sat in front of the Peers' gallery below, where a seat was courteously reserved for him by his brother peers, and for nearly four hours he listened attentively, and apparently with deep interest, to Mr. Gladstone's speech.

It was about 4.25 when Mr. Gladstone entered the House. At that time it was very full—indeed, such was the anxiety to secure comfortable places that many of the members were down as early as three o'clock. The lobby was also full of strangers; but the right honourable gentleman glided by the expectant crowd almost unnoticed. He was there and gone before the few strangers who knew him could recognise him. "That's Gladstone!" some one or two exclaimed, and every eye was turned to see him; but in a moment the right honourable gentleman vanished behind the doors. He did not walk up the floor of the House, but entered behind the Speaker's chair, and proceeded quietly to take his seat; but he was soon recognised, and then a hearty cheer burst from the Ministerial side. The Opposition, we need hardly say, did not cheer heartily. We cannot say that they offered no greetings, for there certainly was a faint cheer, which, being interpreted, seemed to say, "We are glad to see you are recovered from your illness, but what have you got in that red box of yours? We should like to know that before we accord you a hearty greeting."

This was Friday night; and on Friday night, when the adjournment of the House till Monday is moved, there is usually a host of questions to be discussed. On this occasion there were some upon the paper, and among them one standing against the name of Mr. Bernal Osborne; and at the proper time Mr. Bernal Osborne arose to introduce it. Mr. Bernal Osborne is, as we all know, a very acceptable speaker in the House; not that the honourable member has anything very valuable to communicate, for he has not; nor that he ever succeeds in throwing much light upon the subjects on which he speaks. He is rather the rollicking merryman of the House than its teacher; and his speeches are looked upon as comic interludes, pleasant as varieties to relieve the dull tedium of prolonged business, but otherwise of not much value. But on this occasion the House had met for a serious and an important purpose, and was in no humour for fun.

Later in the evening, when the real business of the night was over, Mr. Osborne might have been received with the usual cheers, and a speech from him, as a relief after four hours' tension of the mind, would probably have been hailed as a pleasant relaxation; but just then, when every member was all eye, all ear, all expectation, when the Peers and Commons of England—all the people of England, and, indeed, all Europe—were waiting to know what was to be our future fiscal policy, Mr. Osborne was unanimously voted a bore, as great a bore as an acrobat, Punch and Judy, or an organ-grinder would be opposite the window of the Bank parlour when a financial and commercial crisis is on, and the governors are anxiously debating the propriety of raising the discount another one per cent. And so, when Mr. Osborne rose, instead of being received with the usual cheers and laughter, he met with a storm of "Oh! oh! oh!" so loud and resolute that it cowed even him. "There is a time to be serious, and a time to laugh, Mr. Osborne; this is our serious time." And so Mr. Osborne sat down, not a little chagrined, we may be sure; but, if so, he owed his mortification to himself. How could he dream that the House would hear him, or anybody, when the great Chancellor was there with that ominous box of his before him—that box which by many was expected to prove a horn of plenty, and by others a very Pandora's box, without even hope at the bottom?

Mr. Gladstone rose at about ten minutes to five. By his own side he was again greeted with loud and hearty cheers, while again on the Opposition there only arose here and there a faint and spiritless "Hear, hear!" The right hon. gentleman looked pale and haggard; appeared, moreover, not to be very firm upon his legs, and altogether seemed but little competent to perform the great task that was before him. Dr. Ferguson was under the gallery, and had his eye upon him, and no doubt must have been anxious for his patient as hour after hour he heard his voice and saw him upon his legs, and must have felt relieved when he saw him at last drop into his seat. But there was one present who would be more anxious than Dr. Ferguson, for in the ladies' gallery, peering through the brass screen, sat Mrs. Gladstone; and one can easily imagine how her anxiety would prevail over every other feeling as she watched, and watched, and carefully noted every apparent failure of her husband's voice, and every time that his eloquence was interrupted by his hollow cough.

And now let us notice for a few minutes the appearance of the House as the Chancellor settles himself to his work and unfolds his scheme. He himself, the great orator of the night, stands upright, with his papers before him in the official box, pale and wan, but calm and collected. " What nerves the man must have ! " said a friend to us. And the duty of Mr. Gladstone that night was indeed one that must have taxed his nerves severely ; for it was not merely the House of Commons that was listening, but all Europe ; and, indeed, if we reflect but a moment, we shall see that even future generations were to be addressed that night ; for the words of Mr. Gladstone will not, like most of the words which are uttered here, pass into oblivion as soon as spoken, but will become an historic record, and be read with interest and delight, and quoted as authorities, by ages yet unborn. When the cheering had subsided there was a slight coughing, as if the members were clearing their throats at the beginning that they might not offer any interruption thereafter ; and then there was a rustling, which showed that every man was settling himself down into his easiest position. When the tones of Mr. Gladstone's voice were first heard there were cries of " Order, order ! " to repress the rustling ; and then followed profound silence. And now let us survey the House. Lord Palmerston, you see, settles himself down

into an attitude of the closest attention. He does not lean
back as he often does, but sits sideways, with his face turned
to the Chancellor, and very happy he looks, as if he were
conscious that his Chancellor is about to unfold a scheme of
finance that will do credit to his Government. Lord John
Russell leans backwards, as usual, with his hat over his eyes
and his arms folded across his breast. Sir Charles Wood
stares at the ceiling, and now and then shows signs of approbation by jerking his head, as is his wont. Mr. Sidney
Herbert, as you see, stretches his long legs out before him
and throws his head back upon the edge of the seat, looking
as if he were lying upon an inclined plane, and has an air of
supreme satisfaction. Gladstone and Sidney Herbert are
both disciples of Sir Robert Peel; and, as the Chancellor
further develops the political economy of their great master,
it is not surprising that the Secretary for War should look
pleased. Mr. Milner Gibson is not very demonstrative at
any time; but, as Mr. Gladstone unfolds roll after roll of his
vast scheme—and especially when he comes to the paper
duties—are we wrong in interpreting that look of his as
indicating a quiet inward chuckle? It seems to us as if he
were saying to himself, "Quorum pars magna fui." The
gentleman who sits sideways, with his face towards the
Speaker, at the further end of the Treasury bench, is Mr.
Villiers. We can hardly see his countenance here; but when
we remember how, year after year, before the League was
formed, he attempted to plant the tree of free trade in an
uncongenial soil, we can easily imagine his satisfaction at
seeing, at last, these magnificent results of his patience and
toil. Bright, on the first seat of the second bench below the
gangway, is leaning back and looking upwards, evidently
drinking in with quiet enjoyment every word that is said.
He will himself have something to say on this subject before
it is done with. Sir James Graham, who has lately shifted

from No. 1 below to No. 1 above the gangway, reclines back-
ward and stares into vacancy—very attentive, though, no
doubt. Mr. Hadfield is right behind Sir James, on the top
bench but one. His face is turned towards Gladstone, and
he is unquestionably pleased that his sentiments are making
such progress; for he, too, is an old Freetrader—so free,
indeed, that he wishes to carry out his principles in matters
ecclesiastical as well as fiscal; and sometimes, when the
eloquent Chancellor hits more exactly, in his opinion, the
nail upon the head, he utters a peculiar and expressive
cheer.

On the opposition side of the House the faces were not so
radiant. Some of the members looked unmistakably dis-
pleased, others astonished, whilst on the countenances of
not a few there was a puzzled air, as if the honourable
gentlemen would hardly believe what they heard. Mr.
Disraeli makes no sign. He has his thoughts, no doubt;
but what they are no one can tell from his looks. Sir John
Pakington shows more signs of life, but not much. Mr.
Henley—"Old Henley," as he is here familiarly called—stares
at the speaker from beginning to end with his glass in his eye,
and he neither misses nor will he forget anything, as he will
show you when the time comes. Already, no doubt, he has
noted, or thinks he has, some opening in the panoply of this
formidable foe, into which he hopes to thrust his lance. For
a shrewd and able combatant is " Old Henley," and uncommon cunning of fence, and if there be a weak point in this
Budget we " rede he'll tent it." Lord John Manners is
a very prominent figure upon the Opposition bench. He,
too, has his glass in his eye, through which he steadfastly
gazes upon the speaker, and is evidently puzzled and perplexed—as perplexed as Dame Partlett is when she sees a
duck-chick dabble about in the water. This free trade is not
at all his Lordship's element. Water to an old hen is not

more foreign than Free Trade to a Manners. Ah! my Lord, that "commerce" which you sang about some years ago won't die yet, nor will it kill the "old nobility," but rather strengthen it, if your Lordship and the like of you will but let it. Mr. Walpole is always happy, and always looks the same, "whether he win or lose the game." Sir Bulwer-Lytton is the odd man next to Disraeli, sitting on the very edge of the bench, with his head thrust forward, and making a trumpet of his hand to convey every word to his ear. Strange thoughts and misgivings must haunt Sir Bulwer, for he was a Whig once, but suddenly turned Tory when the battle for Free Trade came on. Ah! Sir Bulwer, you should have stuck to the old ship, and not intrusted your political fortunes to the crazy old barque *Protection*. We don't see Lord Stanley here, but he is present somewhere, we may be sure. His Lordship's is an unhappy case, we consider. His Lordship is currently pronounced a "failure"; and well may this be when, as we know, his aspirations are all one way, whilst a hard destiny has placed him in circumstances which compel him to pull another. There is only one more member of the Opposition whom we can notice, and that is Mr. Bentinck. You see that tall, strongly-built, florid-complexioned man with prominent eyebrows and bushy whiskers, almost a beard, sitting just below the gangway. That is Mr. Bentinck. There are two Mr. Bentincks in the House now, but this is *the* Mr. Bentinck. Mr. Bentinck is a member of the Portland family, representative of a younger branch, and descended from that friend and adviser of Dutch William who came over with his Majesty from Holland at the "glorious revolution." It is many years since the advent of the Dutchman, and the family is unquestionably English now, but in the person of our Mr. Bentinck the Dutch element has certainly come out. You see it in his form, in his face, and in his character. The special feature of Mr.

Bentinck's character is that he never changes his opinion.
All the world may change, and will change, but he never.
As he was in the beginning so he is now, and so he would be
a thousand years hence, if he could live so long. The human
mind, as a rule, is always growing; and change—universal
change—is the law of nature; but there is one thing in the
world, it seems, that is an exception to the rule, and that is
Mr. Bentinck—at least, so he says; and if you look at him
and hear him speak you will be disposed to believe him.
Look at him as he sits opposite Gladstone. Every word he
hears, but no impression is made, you can see. He has been
in the House now eight years; he has in that time seen vast
changes. All the dismal prophecies about the effects of free
trade have failed; all the promises of its advocates have been
realised; 'thousands of Protectionists have been converted,
and the most eloquent champions of monopoly have gradually
been silenced; but there he sits, still unchanged and un-
changeable. And when the debate upon the Budget comes
on we shall hear him uttering the old fallacies and platitudes
with as much solemnity and confidence as he did down in
Norfolk a dozen years ago.

We venture to express a hope that every Englishman will
read Mr. Gladstone's speech. Every Englishman ought to
read it; for it is not only the greatest that Gladstone has
delivered, but it is the greatest that has been delivered by any
one in the House or out of it for many years. In whatever
light we look upon it, it is a great speech. The scheme which
is unfolded is one of the boldest, most comprehensive measures
which have ever been propounded to the English Parliament,
and is fraught with consequences which can never die except
with the nation itself. We do not often offer a political
opinion in these columns, but we cannot help saying that
we look upon this Budget of Gladstone as a magnificent
argosy freighted with untold wealth, which is freely offered

to the people.   The manner in which Gladstone unrolled his
prophetic scroll was something wonderful.   Let our readers
note the marvellous skill that was shown in the gradual evolv-
ing and the grouping of his facts—the artistic way in which
he made every statement seem naturally to lead to what was
to follow—and everything that followed to be the natural
consequence of that which had gone before.   Remark,
further, those little picturesque touches of anecdote which
he every now and then gave us; and, finally, by all means,
let all give themselves up to that magnificent peroration with
which he closed.   The effect of this speech upon the House
was remarkable.   There was but little cheering.   The House
was too deeply absorbed to cheer—too anxious to catch every
word.   For four hours did the great master hold the House
as with a spell.   During that time the dinner hour and the
postal hour came and went, but no one moved; and through
all those hours the House was as silent as a desert.   Not a
whisper nor a rustle was heard—nothing but the clear,
musical voice of the speaker.   Of course, at the close of the
speech there was cheering, hearty, loud, and long-continued,
and no wonder; for cold must have been the nature of the
man who could listen to that marvellous peroration, delivered,
as it was, with almost unequalled power and earnestness,
without being moved.

CHAPTER XIV.

SIR ROBERT PEEL (THE THIRD)—THE LAST DEBATE—KING-
LAKE—SIR ROBERT AGAIN—MR. HORSMAN—MR. WILFRID
LAWSON'S AND MR. STANSFELD'S MAIDEN SPEECHES.

Feb. 25, 1860. IT is impossible to imagine a greater difference between two men than there is between the late Sir Robert Peel and the gentleman who inherits the name, title, and estates of the deceased Baronet. Sir Robert Peel the father was an able, far-seeing, sagacious statesman, an eloquent but discreet orator, a courteous but severely decorous man; a man who never took liberties with any one, and who took care to keep himself within an impassable barrier of étiquette so that no man should take liberties with him. This was Sir Robert the father. How different is Sir Robert the son! The Robert Peel who now exhibits in the House is tall like his father, but there the resemblance ends; there is scarcely anything besides in his form, features, or bearing that reminds you of his parent. As he strides through the lobby he is generally taken by the strangers there to be some distinguished foreigner, and there is certainly something foreign rather than English about him, owing, perhaps, to his having lived much abroad. His figure is tall, imposing, and strikingly well made; his face is handsome and somewhat florid: he wears a thick moustache; his forehead is capacious, but not specially indicative of intellectual power; his eyes are brilliant and restless, and sparkle with waggery, wit, and fun, not unlike some Irish eyes which we have seen.   He dresses in the very best style, not in the extravagance of fashion, but well; and, on the whole, you would take him to be, what we presume he is, a dashing, witty, brilliant man of the world—one who is equally at home on the course, in the gaming-house, in the drawing-room, or at the dinner-table; and we should imagine that his principal characteristics are jollity, humour, wit, reckless audacity, love of fun, and unbounded generosity— regardless of all cost, and perhaps of prudence.   This is the present Sir Robert, a strange son of such a father.

Sir Robert is not a diligent attendant in the House, and has no certain place there.   Sometimes he throws himself on one of the cross-benches below the bar; at other times he sits below the gangway near the Peers' benches, whilst not infrequently he mounts to the highest seat under the members' gallery.   If Sir Robert stays long in the House you may be pretty sure that he means to speak, especially if he have a roll of papers in his hands; and, when it becomes known that he means to favour the House with an exhibition, the young men, and especially the fast young men, will wait for hours for it.   They stop to hear Peel as they would go to a new ballet, or to see the *début* of a prima donna.   These are the young fellows who crowd at the bar and laugh and cheer to the echo when there is any fun going on.   The late Speaker used to look with grave displeasure upon these noisy gatherings, and, occasionally, would call out—" Members at the bar must take their places! " when the crowd would at once scatter and disperse; but the present Speaker seldom, if ever, interferes.   There are not a few, however, in the House who have no sympathy with these noisy exhibitions; but, on the contrary, look upon them as out of place in the English House of Commons.   Especially is this the case,

we apprehend, with the friends of the late Sir Robert.   And
we can easily imagine that it must be painful to see the man
who bears the *clarum et venerabile nomen* of the illustrious
statesman thus condescending to be a sort of oratorical
funambulist to amuse fast young men.   Sir Robert Peel has
a brother in the House, but the two are never seen together.
Nor is this a matter of wonder; for the difference between
these two brothers is quite as great as that between Sir
Robert the father and the present Baronet.   Mr. Frederick
Peel is a dry red-tapist, assiduous and accurate, no doubt;
but never did officialism put on a drier form than that which
it has assumed in the person of Mr. Frederick Peel.   Strange
that these two sons should be so unlike each other—and both
so unlike their father!   We have sometimes thought that all
the passionate part of the late Sir Robert Peel has been con-
densed in his heir, whilst all the plodding assiduity and
accuracy in details which characterised the illustrious Baronet
have been handed down to his younger son; and that, if the
natures of these two could be commingled in one person, the
great statesman might be reproduced.

Sir Robert's exhibition on Friday was, if possible, more
extravagant than it ever had been before.   The subject was
the rifle corps mania; and for the space of half an hour he
kept the House in a roar of laughter.   When, however, we
came to look at the speech, in the *Times*, the next day, it
was difficult to discover why the House thus continuously
laughed—from which we gather that most of the fun must
have been evoked by Sir Robert's manner, while something
of the uproar, no doubt, was owing to the contagious character of mirth; for it is well known that there is nothing
more infectious than laughter.   It is as catching as gaping,
the vapours, and hysterics.   There were, however, two or
three decided hits in Sir Robert's speech which would have
told anywhere.   That image, for instance, of Sir Robert's

corpulent friend crawling for miles upon his belly, or sitting up in a tree for hours. And, again, his advice to the lawyers of the Temple to observe the rule, "in medio tutissimus ibis," which, Sir Robert said, might be translated, "It is safest to stick to the Middle Temple." This last hit tickled Lord Palmerston amazingly. Lord John Russell did not enter into it at first; but when the noble Premier whispered in his ear even his usually immovable face relaxed into a broad grin. It was noticeable that General Peel, the brother of the late Sir Robert, sat a few minutes after his nephew arose, and then got up and quietly left the House—a step which, we think, can surprise nobody.

Mar. 7, 1860. The last debate, on the whole, was not a very vigorous one. The parties were not well matched. Almost all the fighting was on one side. The first night was dreadfully dull—wearisome in the extreme. Du Cane began, and then followed a long list of mediocrities, and during the whole evening not a single speaker of eminence arose. The second night was better, for then we had Bright, with that capital quotation of his; and the third was better still, for Bernal Osborne spoke, Milner Gibson, Gladstone, Disraeli, and " Old Pam." We may finish with Bright's quotation, for, though it has appeared, of course, in the debates, many readers may not have seen it. Here, then, it is :—

"But I have a right to claim the right hon. gentleman the member for Buckinghamshire as a friend to this treaty. (Laughter.) There was a time when he was not the leader of a 'great party.' (Hear, hear.) He was a giant then in another field. He vacated an elevated position there to assume one which is much more laborious. I know not that it is any more useful than that in which he laboured before. (Cheers.) But in one of those very admirable books which the right hon. gentleman wrote, partly for the education, and perhaps rather more for the amusement, of his countrymen—(Hear, hear)—he described the mode of living of an English nobleman of great wealth in Paris. He says: 'Lord Monmouth's dinners at Paris were celebrated. It was generally agreed that they had no rival. Yet there were others who had as skilful cooks—others who, for equal purposes, were as profuse in their expenditure. What was the secret of his success? His Lordship's plates were always hot—(Great laughter); whereas, in Paris in the best-appointed houses, and at dinners, which, for costly materials and admirable art in preparation, cannot be surpassed, the effect is considerably lessened by the fact that every person at dinner is served with a cold plate. (Renewed laughter.) The reason of a custom, or rather a necessity, which one would think a nation so celebrated for their gastronomic tastes would better regulate is that the French porcelain is so inferior that it cannot endure the ordinary heat for dinner.' (Loud laughter.) Now, the right hon. gentleman, with an instinct which we cannot too much admire, breaks out into something like an exclamation. He says: 'Now, if we only had that treaty of commerce with France—(Loud cheers and laughter)—which has been so often on the point of completion, and the fabrics of our unrivalled potteries were given in exchange for their capital wines, the dinners of both nations would be improved. England would gain a delightful beverage, and the French, for the first time in their lives, would dine off hot plates." (Roars of laughter.) And he concludes with an expression which I recommend to his devoted followers—' An unanswerable instance of the advantages of commercial reciprocity.' " (Prolonged cheers and laughter.)

No language can describe the laughter that followed. We do believe that the House might have been heard in Palace-yard. Disraeli himself could not withstand the infection, for even he actually smiled.

Mar. 16, 1860. Last week we had a short debate on the question of the annexation of Savoy, which we feel bound to notice ; first to introduce to our readers Mr. Kinglake, the celebrated author of " Eöthen" ; and secondly to call attention to the remarkable change which has lately come over Sir Robert Peel. Of Mr. Kinglake we have to report that he never can achieve a Parliamentary success. His fame as an author he has established, and with that he must be contented, for as a speaker in the House he never can be remarkable. The honourable gentleman has fine talents and great genius, but he lacks physical power ever to address the House with effect. His speech on this occasion may be aptly described as forcibly-feeble, but not in the sense in which this phrase is commonly used, for it is generally applied to men whose language and manners are forcible, whilst their matter is feeble. It is the loud-tongued, dramatic utterers of empty nothings that this epithet usually describes; but Mr. Kinglake is not one of this class. On the contrary, his matter is good and forcible; it is his manner that is feeble; and it ever must be so, for, as we have said, Mr. Kinglake has not, and never can have, the physical qualifications necessary to make a speaker. He is short in stature, very near-sighted, feeble in voice, and apparently generally weak in constitution. Mr. King-lake's want of success as a speaker is to be regretted for his own sake and for the sake of the country; for the honourable gentleman, no doubt, feels that he has something to say, and is moved by a laudable ambition to express his thoughts. And we, too, who have read his book, know that whatever the honourable gentleman thinks is worthy of being expressed, and must ever regret that he cannot speak his thoughts as well as he can write them.

A fortnight ago we noticed in terms of censure the oratorical escapades of Sir Robert Peel: we feel, therefore, bound in justice to the honourable Baronet to call special attention to the remarkable speech which he delivered on this occasion. Since we last wrote a great change has come over Sir Robert, so great that it may be called in Puritan phrase " a conversion," " a newness of life." When the afflatus descended upon the honourable Baronet we have not learned, nor do we know whether it was the result of re-flection or was a sudden inspiration; but that he has been the subject of something analogous to " a new birth " is patent. Sir Robert Peel has been in the House of Commons nearly ten years, for he was first returned on the death of his father in July, 1850; but during the whole of this period Sir Robert never did anything worthy of his name until last week. Men, indeed, had generally come to the con-

clusion that, though he was known to possess talent of no
mean order, he would never rise to a higher position than
that of a rollicking, witty, amusing speaker. But on this
occasion the honourable Baronet disappointed all these
prophecies, and delivered a speech which, whether we consider the sentiments uttered, the eloquent language in which
they were delivered, or the striking and appropriate manner
with which they were enforced, we must decide was one of
the most successful efforts of modern days. Sir Robert
arose when the House was full, and when he arose the
lovers of fun of course expected an exhibition, though it was
dfficult to see how Sir Robert could excite merriment on so
serious a subject; whilst the sober, serious men evidently
were in doubt—sat, as we may say, upon thorns—lest Sir
Robert should mar the discussion of so grave a matter by
ill-timed buffoonery and wit. The honourable gentleman,
however, soon disappointed the young men, and set at rest
all the anxieties of the old. The attention of the House
whilst Sir Robert was speaking was just that sort of attention which we love to see in the House. It was serious—
devout, we might almost say—and when the House broke
out into a cheer it was clearly the expression of the deep
feeling of manly English hearts. How different was all this
from the loud, boisterous "yah! yahs!" of the rollicking
fast men who have usually greeted the honourable Baronet;
and how much more pleasant a subject for reflection must
this effect have been to Sir Robert himself!

Every one who is experienced in the manners of the
House knows well the distinctions in the cheering of its
members. In addition to the uproarious cheering, mixed
with laughter, which Sir Robert used to call forth, there is
the defiant cheer more like a yell than a cheer. This is
most commonly heard from the Conservative side of the
House. When Lord John Manners was pitching into Bright

the other night there was a perfect storm of this sort of cheering. Then there is the cheer derisive, which is very expressive; and, again, the cheer confirmatory. Thus, when an honourable member charges another with having uttered some sentiments which, in the opinion of the speaker, were flagrantly wrong, the friends of the member attacked will break out into a confirmatory cheer, which, being interpreted, means, "Yes, he did say it, and what he said is true." There is also the obstructive cheer, of which we shall have an opportunity of saying something by and by; and, lastly, there is the genuine English, manly, approving cheer. It was this sort of cheering that Sir Robert Peel evoked on this occasion—a manly, hearty, generous cheer burst forth into what is called overwhelming applause when he sat down. No doubt this cheering was inspired by the sentiments which he uttered, as we have said; but are we wrong in supposing that it was also coloured with a feeling of delight that it was the man who bears the honoured name of "Sir Robert Peel" that had uttered them? We, of course, could not cheer, for if we had opened our lips we should have probably caught the attention of the Sergeant-at-Arms, and been compelled to descend from the gallery and do penance at the bar; but we confess that if we had broken loose it would have been quite as much from a feeling of delight that it was Sir Robert Peel who was speaking as from approbation of what he said. Sir Robert Peel, then, has gained a new position in the House, and straight before him there lies open a noble and honourable career. Will he pursue it? We cannot allow ourselves to harbour a doubt that he will. He has felt his power. Up to the other day Sir Robert aspired to no higher position than that of amusing the House, and perhaps did not feel that he was capable of a loftier flight. He has now, however, taken a nobler position. He has arrested the serious

attention and stirred the hearts of the English Commons.
He has gained the respect and approbation of men whose
respect and approval are worth seeking; and, what is even
better still, he has doubtless gained his own; and until we
have seen to the contrary we will not believe that he can
give up the high and honourable position which he has
achieved.   Sir Robert is endowed with all the qualifications
of a good speaker; he has excellent abilities, fine voice, commanding appearance, and, when he will, he can use the
advantages which he possesses with effect.   That he has
wit at command we know too well; but he has also humour,
which is a much higher quality than mere sparkling wit.
There is no reason why he should entirely forego these latter
advantages; they, too, were given to be used; but he must
make them his servants, and not let them be his masters.
Wit and humour are not out of place even in the House of
Commons, but they should be used sparingly for the purpose
of illustrating and enforcing the matter in hand, and not
with the intention prepense of turning the House of
Commons' proceedings into farcical exhibitions; in short, in
such a place, and in all similar places, the comic element
should be kept well in hand, and "within the limits of
becoming mirth."

Mar. 17, 1860.   There is a universal feeling in the House that
there is no sincerity at the bottom of all Mr.
Horsman's solemn and earnest harangues.   There is the
appearance of it; for no man in the House speaks with
such signs of solemn and earnest conviction as he.   At
times he seems to be almost overpowered by the force of
his convictions, and his manner and the tone of his voice
are more those of the pulpit than of the senate-house.
But still, all this notwithstanding, the feeling alluded to
prevails.   Members listen and applaud, and then say, "Ah!

it's all very well; but he would be just as solemn and earnest on the other side if it suited his purpose." " That was a fine speech of Horsman's," said one member to another from the " green isle." " True," said the other, " it was a fine speech, and a very able speech; but there was one great fault about it." " What was that?" " Why, he doesn't believe a word of it; and if Lord Palmerston had given him the seat in the Cabinet which he wanted he would have spoken just as seriously the other way." Every one felt that this was so when Mr. Horsman spoke on the French commercial treaty. Of the subject of coals he knew nothing himself; but he wanted to damage the Government; and as, according to the proverb, " any stick will do to beat a dog," he took up the subject of the probable exhaustion of our coal mines, not understanding the subject, nor believing in his own figures, nor, indeed, caring at all about the matter.

But Mr. Horsman fell into a trap. He calculated upon the ignorance of his audience, and made a mistake. Most of them were, no doubt, profoundly ignorant; but there was one that was not. Behind Mr. Horsman sat Mr. Hussey Vivian; and whilst Mr. Horsman was speaking Mr. Vivian must have chuckled with delight to see Mr. Horsman stumbling from blunder to blunder as he did, whilst he (Mr. Vivian) had in his hands or in his memory the refutation of all the right honourable gentleman's mistakes. Mr. Hussey Vivian has been in the House eight years, and, until that night, had never made a speech, and probably was not at all sure that he could make one. But occasions make men. For years Mr. Vivian had studied the subject, not as a theorist, but as a practical man largely interested in coal-fields, and, seeing this notice which Mr. Horsman had put upon the paper, he was suddenly inspired to bring his know-ledge and experience to bear; and he did it, and did it well. At first he was nervous and shaky, but the House came to his rescue. It found that he had something to say, and, according to its wont, it encouraged him to say it; and Mr. Vivian proceeded, calmly and coolly, to deliver a speech which, as an answer to Mr. Horsman, was one of the most conclusive and effective speeches heard that evening. " It took up Mr. Horsman's bag of theories," as a member said, " and turned it inside out, and shook it, and then filled it again with substantial facts."

Mar. 31, 1860. From the bottom of our hearts we pitied Mr. Wilfrid Lawson when he arose to deliver his maiden speech to the House. Mr. Lawson is the son of a daughter of the late Sir James Graham, and therefore the present Sir James's nephew. He is also the colleague of Sir James in the representation of Carlisle, which place he was elected to represent in Parliament in 1859. But, though thus nearly related to the " Netherby Knight" by blood, there cannot be much political sympathy between him and his uncle; for Mr. Lawson is a Radical of the advanced school, whereas Sir James, whatever he may be just now, is certainly not that. Well, on the night when Mr. Berkeley brought in his customary bill for the Ballot, Mr. Lawson determined to deliver his maiden speech. It was a ticklish time for Mr. Lawson, no doubt, and one to which he had looked forward with no small anxiety; but still there were not wanting encouragements. First, he knew that it is the practice of the House always to listen with courtesy and patience to a new member; secondly, he was not an unpractised speaker; for, though he had not before spoken in the House, he had often addressed popular assemblies outside, and with success; and, thirdly, he was well prepared, had studied his subject, arranged his arguments, and set his notes in due order. But, alas! Mr. Wilfrid Lawson had reckoned without his host. There was one thing which he had for-

gotten, and on this he was wrecked. He had forgotten that
he might possibly have to rise near the dinner hour, and that
when men are rabidly hungry they are never courteous. It
was past seven when Mr. Lawson arose, and for some time
the House had been restless and noisy. Hardly would it
listen to Mr. Marsh whilst he showed how the Ballot had
failed in Australia. Still less courtesy did it award to Mr.
Fortescue when he spoke; and when Mr. Lawson arose,
though there were faint cries of "New member!" its
patience was utterly exhausted. Nor is this surprising.
Usually the House is very courteous to new members;
but hunger, all over the world, overrides courtesy. At
the moment when Mr. Lawson arose a hundred tables—
in the dining-room, at the clubs, and in private houses—
were decked with damask and plate; a hundred cooks
were looking with anxiety to their spits, and waiting
impatiently for the signal "to dish"; and twice a hundred
obsequious flunkies were at their posts, listening for the
carriage wheels and the impetuous knock of masters and
guests. And, more than this, here were actually present
between 300 and 400 hungry men, who knew all this, and,
more impatient than cooks and flunkies, were anxious to
rush away and dine. Is it wonderful, then, that when Mr.
Lawson arose all the courtesy which usually waits upon
new members failed? Not at all. Men will, as we know
from scores of fearful narratives, eat one another when
hard pressed by hunger. "Why, hang it!" said a score
of loungers in the lobby and at the bar, "here's another
man up." Who is he?" "Why, it's 'Old Jemmy's'
nephew.' And they say he's a new member, and we
must hear him." "Oh, hang your new member! He
should choose a better time; are we to have our dinner
spoiled through his impertinence? Come, let us put him
down." And so the row began; and what a row! It

began at the bar; it was echoed from the back of the chair, where other impatient malcontents had clustered; it was taken up all along the Conservative benches. Even on Mr. Lawson's own side of the House it was not less furious; and from the galleries above it poured down upon his head. It was not merely a cry of " Divide, 'vide, 'vide ! " but a regular storm of groans, and cheers, and laughter, and indescribable noises. For a time Mr. Lawson stood it bravely, occasionally speaking, and at other times looking round with a sort of deprecatory and imploring look; but it was of no use. When he spoke his words were drowned in the storm, and bursts of laughter met his patient and imploring looks. And so, in about five minutes, the hon. member wisely sat down, pocketed his notes, and postponed his *début* as a speaker to a more favourable time. We, however, who quietly marked the hon. member in the midst of this noisy scene, augur favourably of him; for we could not help noting that Mr. Lawson possesses at least one qualification necessary to a speaker in the House —namely, calm self-possession.

On Thursday we had another maiden speech, and a much more successful one. The *débutant* on this occasion was Mr. Stansfeld. He also is a new member, one of the creations of the last general election. Mr. Stansfeld is member for the town of Halifax, where he was born, but he lives at Walham-green, and has forsaken the Bar to brew beer for the citizens of London. Mr. Stansfeld is also a Radical of the advanced sort. He is specially known, however, amongst the workers for Italian liberty as the fast friend of Mazzini. The Italian Republican chief, we believe, lives with Mr. Stansfeld. It is too soon to prognosticate that Mr. Stansfeld will become a power in the House of Commons; it is difficult to judge from first attempts. Many a speaker has failed at first and succeeded afterwards; whilst not a few have made tolerably good first speeches, and thus have raised hopes which their subsequent attempts have not justified. Mr. Stansfeld's first speech must be considered a success. His ease and self-possession seemed to be perfect. What he meant to say he succeeded in saying, which is a great success to achieve in a maiden speech. His manner was easy and unaffected, if not very impressive; whilst as to his matter, if there were no very strong points, nor anything profound or new, there was certainly nothing puerile or weak. In the House Mr. Stansfeld's first attempt at speaking was universally adjudged as having been very successful. Sir John Pakington, who followed, characterised the speech as one of great ability, and in private the congratulations which the honourable member received were hearty and numerous.

CHAPTER XV.

April 28, 1860. EVER since the great fight "two voices" have been talking within us—one urging that we should say nothing about that event; the other, with equal pertinacity, moving us to speak. "I would not say anything about that fight if I were you," said the first. "Why not?" said the second. "Oh, it is such a low, vulgar affair; and it is not right that the people of England should think that their 'conscript fathers' have taken an interest in such a disreputable business." "But they did take an interest in it." "Yes, I know; but it is not worth while to let the people know this. Will it not tend to lower the august assembly in the public mind?" "But we write the 'Inner Life,' remember, and how can we in conscience conceal it from our readers?" "Ah, to be sure! but as the sons of Noah threw a robe over their father when they discovered him in the cave, so I would advise that you should cast a veil over the weakness of the House." But to this the second voice replied "No! It is best to be honest. Besides, is it so guilty a thing to do—to read about, and take an interest in, this fight? If so, verily we are all guilty; for rely upon it that from the throne to the

143

cottage, and lower still, all felt more or less interested in this fight." Whereupon Voice 1 uttered a deep sigh, and was silent.

Yes, it is so. It cannot be denied. From the highest to the lowest—peers and paupers—high dignitaries of the law and high dignitaries of the church—the clergy, established and dissenting—religious people and irreligious—all, more or less, have been moved by this event. Why, then, should we conceal the fact that here also the all-pervading excitement was felt? We see no reason, and, therefore, shall proceed. Well, then, here, as everywhere else, the fight between Heenan and Sayers for several days was the engrossing topic of all conversation. You might see by the earnestness of strangers in the lobby that they had caught the mania. Sometimes, indeed, they suited the action to the word, as the orators inside are wont to do, and tried to show, as well as to narrate, how the battle was fought. In the division lobbies all day on Wednesday hon. members clustered in knots to discuss this subject, and every man who had been present at the fight was the centre of a circle of anxious inquirers; and, even in the House itself, whilst professedly engaged in the business of legislation, hon. members in an undertone were really debating the respective merits of the Champion and the Benicia Boy.

On Friday night the subject of the fight was formally brought before the House. Mr. W. Ewart, the member for Dumfries, was the interpellator, and he introduced his question to the Home Secretary with a speech. Mr. William Ewart is well known in the House as a social reformer. He goes in for the elevation of the people—advocates the establishment of local libraries, parks, and pleasure-grounds; and it was therefore appropriate for him to seek to put down this sort of "brutalising exhibition." But the hon. member did not take much by his move. It was not well timed. He should have waited a week or two, when possibly the House will have returned to its right mind. The hon. gentleman talked for about a quarter of an hour, but very little of what he said was heard, and the ironical cheers with which he was greeted showed unmistakably that the House was not in the mood to be improved by his sermon.

When he sat down Mr. Vincent Scully rose, and was received with loud cheers. Mr. Scully is an Irishman, with more than the usual dash of Irish humour in him, and is therefore generally received with mirth when he rises to address the House. On this occasion the expectation of amusement was fully justified, for, to the surprise of everybody, he, too, had a lecture to deliver on this "outrage on public morals." Coming from an Irishman this was droll enough; but when Mr. Scully said that in Ireland such exhibitions would not be tolerated, and expressed a hope that the Home Secretary would treat the subject in a serious manner, the mirth of the House became uncontrollable.

At last the Home Secretary rose, and in a moment the House became quiet. The Home Secretary is the deity who presides over the police of the nation, and the fight, therefore, came properly within the cognisance of his department; and when he came from behind his cloud it was expected that his deliverance on the question would be very solemn and serious. The disapprovers of the fight anticipated a smile of encouragement; those who sanctioned it expected to be transfixed by a frown. No wonder, then, that when Sir George Cornewall Lewis rose a solemn silence pervaded the House. But Sir George Lewis disappointed all the expectations which were entertained; for he neither blessed the opponents of prize-fights with a smile nor transfixed the advocates with a frown. Nor did he take exactly a middle course. Indeed, beneath his carefully studied language it was easy to see that, whilst he was not prepared to sanction pugilistic encounters, he was certainly not inclined to pour out upon them the vials of his divine wrath. If by office he is divine, he showed that by nature he is human. Of course, occupying the high position which he fills, he could not directly defend prize-fights; he therefore showed the House how the advocates defended them. "It was said" (such was the artful manner in which the Home Secretary delivered himself) "that the pugilistic encounter afforded a model of fair fighting. It was said that it afforded an inducement to practise a mode of fighting better than the use of the bowie-knife or the stiletto, or that other mode of fighting not uncommon in Ireland—viz., with the shillelagh." The allusion to the bowie-knife was one for America's nob. The mention of the stiletto pointed at Italy; whilst the allusion to the shillelagh was directed at Mr. Scully. This part of Sir George's speech was loudly cheered by the partisans of the ring, and especially the latter part of it. Here the cheers and laughter made the walls echo again; and the gravity of the serious part of the House—including Mr. Scully—was disturbed. On the whole, then, the impression was, that so intense had been the interest felt in the fight that even the gods themselves were moved, as of old they used to be (see Homer, Virgil, &c.), if not to take part in it, to look down with feelings of anything but disapproval. And, after this, what could be said on the question? When Sir George had finished the majority of the members rose like a flock of birds, and, as they sped away, chuckled merrily over the result of Mr. Ewart's questions. But we must not neglect here to note one singular fact. Whilst Sir George was speaking it was observed that a humorous smile irradiated his face. Those who know Sir George will be struck with this as a remarkable phenomenon.

And what did the members proceed to do? Shall we

divulge it? Why not, after such a speech as that of Sir
George Cornewall Lewis? Well, then, some few of the
faster sort stationed themselves in the division lobby and
levied toll upon the passers-by for the benefit of Tom Sayers;
and they were very successful in their exactions, for before
the night closed upwards of seventy honourable members had
subscribed a sovereign each, and since then the number has,
we learn, increased to a hundred. Now, here is a fine
opportunity for a moral sermon. And there are not wanting
materials for an exceedingly eloquent and edifying discourse.
We might contrast the beginning and ending of this episode
—how it commenced with the Speaker at the table, the robed
chaplain at his side, and the members with their faces turned
to the wall, all solemnly engaged in prayer; and how it
finished with a collection for a prize-fighter. We might
also summon up those solemn old Puritan members of
the Long Parliament — Cromwell, Hampden, Pym, and
others—to frown upon these proceedings; and might dwell
largely on the degeneracy of the modern House as compared
with that sturdy Puritan race. But we forbear, for in truth
we are in no mood now to moralise; for we frankly confess
that we, too, have eaten of the insane root and partaken with
the ungodly of this widespread excitement. We are almost
ashamed of it; but so it is, and there we must leave it.

May 5, 1860. On Thursday night, when the order for the
adjourned debate on the second reading of
the Reform Bill stood first on the paper, it was known
that Sir Edward Bulwer-Lytton intended to deliver an
oration, which for several days he had been studying
and moulding into form, and hence at an early hour
the house was well filled. It will be remembered that
when Sir Edward was Colonial Secretary in the Derby
Government his health failed, and then very mournful

forebodings were whispered in the clubs and lobbies that
we should probably never hear Sir Edward's voice again in
Parliament. We have, however, now to report, and it is with
great pleasure that we do so, that these forebodings have
all been falsified, and that the right hon. Baronet is quite
well—looks, indeed, better than we have seen him for some
years past; further, we notice that he has divested his
face of some of the shaggy hirsute disfigurements which
he used to delight in; and still again, that he has wonderfully improved in his manner and action. Sir Edward's
action whilst speaking used to be most extraordinary,
grotesque, and ungainly. He would throw himself backwards until you would imagine that he must fall to his
seat, and again would bend his body forward like a dervish
performing his devotions. All this he has, however, altered,
and his action is modest and graceful compared with
what it was, although it is still much more energetic and
various than that of any other speaker in the House, always
excepting Mr. Whiteside, whose gesticulation is more extravagant than can be conceived by any one who has not seen
that hon. gentleman "on his legs." On the whole, then, Sir
Edward as an orator is wonderfully altered. The clipping
and singeing which he has undergone has greatly improved
his personal appearance, and the moderating of his gesticulation has added considerably to the effect of his delivery. But
still there is one fault left, which does and must ever, unless
it can be got over, detract from the power and effectiveness
of his speaking—we mean the incapacity under which he
suffers to modulate properly his voice, so far as modulation
means inflecting or varying the tone. Sir Edward has the
power of modulation, for the fault which we complain of is
that he varies and inflects too much, too violently we may
say; for sometimes he shouts out at the top of his voice, and
anon he sinks it into something very much like a whisper;

and the effect is that when he speaks loudly his words
at the close of his sentences become merely inarticulate
sounds, and when he sinks his voice he is to most of the
members, especially to the elder ones, inaudible. The cause
of this is not far to seek—the right hon. Baronet is distress-
ingly deaf. Not only is it difficult for him to hear what
others say to him, but he cannot hear well what he says to
others. Hence it is obvious that it is impossible that he can
vary and inflect his voice with that nice perception which is
so necessary to an orator. A pianoforte-player might play,
perhaps, effectively, even though he were deaf; Beethoven,
we know, did long after he had ceased to hear. But how
would it be with a violin-player, who depends upon nicety of
ear quite as much as upon delicacy of touch to produce the
right sound? It is remarkable that in the gallery we seem to
have heard Sir Edward better than the members below, but
the reporters there were often grievously at fault, and frequently had to guess at some of the right hon. Baronet's
words. More than one member left the House in despair
and wandered about the lobby, and when asked why they
did not go in, replied that they must read the speech, for
they could not hear it.

It has been over and over again said that this speech
of Sir Edward's was "a great speech." "Did you hear
Bulwer's speech?" was a question often put during the
evening. "Yes; and a magnificent speech it was—the
greatest speech which I ever heard him deliver," was generally the reply. "I think," said one enthusiastic Conservative,
"that it was one of the greatest speeches that ever were
delivered in the House." And in many senses it was "a
great speech." It was long, and, in the opinion of not a
few, length is an important element of a great speech. It
was got up, moreover, with great care. Many hours had,
no doubt, been spent by Sir Edward over this oration. The

topics of the speech were well arranged ; the rhetoric was perfect ; the sentences were composed with as much care as an Etonian gives to his Latin verses.   Every word seemed to have been accurately examined and weighed before it was adopted, and the language was that of an accomplished and long-practised writer ; but, when we come to read the speech as we find it in the *Times*, we do not discover much that is new in it.   It is simply a rehash of old objections to the extension of the franchise elegantly served up.   The objections may be true (upon this subject we offer no opinion here), but they are certainly not new.   There were no thoughts which hang by you and will not away ; nor any of those beautiful illustrations which we find in the speeches of the old masters of oratory, which haunt the memory like some of the melodies of Beethoven and Mozart.   On the whole, then, we decide that, if this was a great speech, it was only so for these times, and not for all time : great because it stands out well amongst the vulgar littlenesses which are so common now, but not essentially and truly great.

June 9, 1860.   "The thunder of Demosthenes" has become a settled phrase ; and no doubt Demosthenes was a real thunderer, and when he

> "Shook the arsenal
> And fulmined over Greece,"

it was no stage trick ; but there have not been many real oratorical thunderers in the world, and especially in modern times.   There were some in the Long Parliament, though they did not indulge in protracted roars, but rather in short, sharp, explosive claps, which are said to be more dangerous.   At all events, the Puritan thunder was wonderfully effective, as we know.   Mirabeau, too, was a genuine thunderer, and Danton ; but since them there have been very few thunderers indeed. Brougham, we take it, was genuine; for that could not have been a mimetic bolt which made Canning jump from his seat and shout in excited tones, " It is false ! " In these days we have no thunderers—literally none. Disraeli sometimes tries to come the thunderer, but he does not succeed; and never did he fail more decidedly than he did on Monday night when he spoke on Lord John Russell's Reform Bill. That he meant to be very grand and effective there is no doubt. All his manner showed that he intended to thunder, and transfix Lord John with a fatal bolt. He began in that peculiar calm way of his which he always adopts when he means mischief. He walked up to the table quietly; he pulled down his waistcoat; he adjusted his coat-sleeves; he thrust his hands into his trousers pockets. At first his language was rather complimentary than otherwise. Disraeli often preludes a tremendous attack with oily compliments—like the boa-constrictor licking the animal that he means to devour. But gradually he becomes more excited, and at length he got into a more furious rage than we ever saw him in before. He threw his arms about; he clenched his fist and shook it passionately at the noble Lord opposite, and he shrieked so loudly that his voice was heard in the outer lobby. But there was evidently no reality in all this. It was clearly "pumped thunder"—nothing more. It was prompted by no real feeling; it was inspired by no real anger. We have heard Brougham in the House, years ago; and when he thundered we, in common with all present, have held our breath and felt creep over us a cold shudder, as he gathered up his strength to hurl his bolts. But nobody felt this or anything like it when Disraeli was speaking on Monday night. The Conservatives—the few of them that stopped (for be it known that in the midst of all this storm many of them crawled away to dinner)—cheered uproariously; but the cheers were, like the thunder, pumped, and not genuine and hearty.   And as to Lord John, who was the object at which the orator was aiming, so far from being frightened, and awed, and cowed, he sat on the Treasury bench and smiled.   When Disraeli sat down nobody with excited manner and hurried tones got up to answer him ; but, just as if nothing had happened, the next business was called, and Mr. Mackinnon arose and introduced his motion. In short, one actor left the stage, the scene shifted, and another actor came on.   Yes, it was mere acting; not " Heaven's own artillery," all this noise, but pumped thunder—nothing more.

Sept. 1, 1860. The Session of 1860 is at an end.   It has been the longest Session which we have had for many years.   It began on Tuesday, January 24; it finished on Tuesday, August 28 : lasting thirty-one weeks and one day.   And not only has it been the longest but the severest of modern Sessions.   Indeed, it may be questioned whether the House of Commons has ever before in one Session sat so many hours.   In the earlier part of the Session—about the first week or so—the House occasionally rose before twelve; but since then, as a rule, it has sat on till two o'clock, often till three, and in several instances it touched upon four in the morning.   The labour of the Session, therefore, has been exceedingly severe.   Fortunately, however, the weather has not been oppressively hot, and the Thames has been unusually inodorous ; otherwise the officers of the House, and the members of the Government who were obliged to be present, would certainly have broken down ; we must except, however, Lord Palmerston, for upon him neither labour nor weather seems to make the smallest impression. He enters the House soon after it meets ; he stops, as a rule, till it closes, and then walks away seemingly as fresh as he

was when he came. Some people wonder when he eats and
sleeps. The answer is, he eats and sleeps on the premises—
eats at the restaurant; sleeps on the benches. The noble
Lord apparently has the power to sleep at will. When a
long-winded orator rises he can fold his arms, and at once,
without effort, enter the land of dreams; when another gets
up whom he wishes to hear, he can, with equal facility, shake
off his sleep. He has no occasion to court Sleep, for she is
always ready to welcome him, and he has no trouble in getting
rid of her. Suddenly he falls asleep when he wishes, and
suddenly, when required to be so, he is wide awake, attentive,
and ready to speak, and, what is more remarkable, he seems
to lose nothing by his sleep; for in his winding-up speeches,
as we have often noticed, every point of importance is touched
upon, every false statement is corrected, and not an argument
of any weight is left unanswered. All this is owing, no doubt,
to habit and long experience. His experience tells him when
he can go to sleep in safety; by habit he has become enabled
to sleep and wake at will. When a Darby Griffith rises, for
example, his Lordship knows he may go off quietly into a
snooze; and so long as the soothing ripple of Mr. Griffith's
eloquence continues to flow the noble Lord continues sleeping; probably it lulls rather than disturbs him, just as the
quiet murmur of a brook soothes a tired rustic on its banks.
We have ourselves found it have this effect. But if, when
Griffith sits down, Disraeli should rise, the charm is broken
in a moment, and at once the noble Lord is all ear and
attention. It is a wonderful faculty, this, of sleeping and
waking at will, and very useful to the noble Lord; but to
others who have it not it is disadvantageous, for it makes the
noble Lord—to the great distress of those who cannot sleep
and wake at will—careless of the prolongation of the sitting
of the House. We ourselves have often wished that the
noble Lord were like unto other men. It has long been

noticed in the House that when Lord Palmerston is leader of the Government we always sit late, whilst Lord John Russell and Disraeli are averse from long sittings. It is rumoured that next Session a resolute attempt will be made to put a stop to these late sittings. The members who cannot stop have become jealous of them, as well they may be, for it often happens that measures in which they take a deep interest are smuggled through the House when they are quietly in bed. Indeed, there has arisen a general outcry against them. The reporters in the gallery have long since silently expressed their view of the matter, for it will have been observed that nothing has been reported at length during the past Session after about one o'clock. Let us hope, then, that next Session we shall have a reform. It may be easily accomplished. Two or three resolute men— or even one—might effectually stop all business at a certain hour.

"Well, it has been a barren Session, a fruitless Session, a blank Session, after all. Those chattering members have sat long, but have done nothing. The mountain has laboured, and has brought nothing forth but a ridiculous mouse." Thus grumble, no doubt, nine-tenths of our readers, for thus barks the *Times*, and thus, in chorus, has barked all the daily, weekly, metropolitan, and provincial press. But the verdict is not true, nevertheless. On the contrary, the Session has been anything but barren. Parliament has, it is true, not done the work which was given it to do, but it has got through a marvellous amount of labour; and when the historian shall sum up the results of the Session of 1860 it will be found to have been a long way from fruitless. For instance, it has accepted and ratified the French Treaty, and passed all the measures springing therefrom. It has voted about £72,000,000 of money; it has decided upon fortifying our dockyards, &c.; it has abolished the Indian Army; it has reformed the naval code of laws; and, altogether, it has passed about 100 *public and some* 250 *private Bills.* Even this, however, is by no means the extent of its labours, for it has split itself up into Committees, and in a few weeks at least a dozen blue-books will testify against the cry that this has been a barren Session. Upon the value of its labours, whether the measures which Parliament has passed be good or bad, we offer no opinion here; but that it was worked hard and with large results we must affirm against all comers.

Mar. 28, 1861. What is the matter with Mr. Disraeli? Is he dyspeptic, that he has lately shown such signs of irritability? Or does the state of affairs behind annoy him? The open revolt of the sturdy and uncompromising Bentinck, who is evidently kicking against Caucasian rule, and seems determined to set up on his own hook; and the jealousies, and antagonisms, and contrarieties which appear to be flowing out of Italian affairs—we know not what it is; but it is evident that something frets him, for lately he has on more than one occasion shown a sensitiveness which he had never shown before. For example, a week or two ago he rose, and, in excited tones, called the Home Secretary over the coals because some Bill which was down upon the paper had not been brought on, and wanted to know when it would be brought on. "It was announced that it was to be taken that night. Hon. members had waited in considerable numbers for the Bill. Why was it again postponed? When would it really be taken? Such a loose management of public affairs was exceedingly inconvenient," &c. Hon. members stared at this explosion, and wondered what it meant. "Has the worthy Home Secretary, usually so methodical and frank in his business arrangements, and so willing in all his plans to make things agreeable to foes as well as friends, really been guilty of some mistake?" What can it mean? Our surprise was still further increased when Sir George, in his calm way, called the attention of the right hon. gentleman to the fact that he (Sir George) had positively announced on the Monday preceding that the Bill would not come on, but would only be put down on the paper that he might fix a convenient day for its discussion. Again, there was that singular episode of Friday night. The gallant, gay, and somewhat reckless, roving Sir Robert Peel was speaking and, thinking that Mr. Disraeli was smiling at something which he had said, took the liberty of remarking "that the right hon. member for Buckinghamshire seemed to be excessively amused;" whereupon up jumped the right hon. gentleman "to order," and rebuked the hon. Baronet for his impertinence. Now, no doubt, Sir Robert was mistaken; and, possibly, by a little stretching of the standing rules of debate, he might be deemed to be out of order. But surely it was hardly worth notice, and not a little *infra dig.*, for a man in Mr. Disraeli's position to notice it. And here we may express our curiosity to know what Mr. Speaker would have done if Sir Robert had continued to refuse an apology. "I do not see," said Sir Robert, "that the remark of Mr. Speaker calls for any observation." "Then," said Mr. Speaker, "I shall feel it necessary to express a more decided opinion." Query, what opinion would he have expressed? All this, to us, seems to be very small—invoking the thunder of the gods to kill a fly. Mr. Disraeli probably did not smile at all: we should say he certainly did not, for he seldom smiles. But no sin would have been committed if he had. Nor do we see that Sir Robert's allusion, mistaken though he was, called for Mr. Disraeli's denial, or the rebuke of Mr. Speaker.

April 20, 1861. Monday was the great Budget night, and such was the anxiety to hear the Chancellor of the

Exchequer unfold his financial scheme, that as early as ten o'clock in the morning St. Stephen's gateway was lined with strangers having orders, come thus early to be sure of admission. The House opens at four; these gentlemen had therefore to wearily wait, seated upon the bare stone benches, for six hours. Surely the mania outside the House to hear a speech is stronger even than the mania inside to make one. At four o'clock the House was full, and the lobby was so crowded that it was not without difficulty that the sturdy superintendent of the police and his force could keep a narrow lane clear for the members to pass. "Under the gallery," where the Peers have a right to places, was so packed that the biggest of wigs had to stand. Thus, for example, the Bishop of London could nowhere find a seat, nor the Lord Chancellor, nor even the Commander-in-chief of her Majesty's forces, his Royal Highness the Duke of Cambridge, but were obliged to stand in a narrow gangway and look over one another's shoulders as well as they could. They came late, the Royal and noble representatives of the Army, the Church, and the Law, and thus paid the penalty of their want of punctuality. At half-past four Gladstone tripped through the crowd, took his green box, "big with fate," from the doorkeeper, and entered the House; and in a few minutes afterwards he was upon his legs opening his Budget, with the House thronged, and some thousand eyes fixed upon him, and some thousand ears open to devour his words. The silence was as of the grave; the anxiety was intense. And what wonder when we consider that of that closely packed assembly of over 700 men (including strangers) not ten, probably, knew that box's contents which the Chancellor was about to expose. The Conservatives hoped, the Liberals feared, that he would have a deficiency. Indeed this was pretty confidently expected by all parties, both inside and outside; and even up to the last the question asked was,

not what will be done with the surplus, but how will
Gladstone provide for the deficiency? The Liberals asked
the question with dismay—the Conservatives with triumph,
hoping to get the Chancellor of the Exchequer upon the hip,
and perhaps oust him from the Government. "I don't see,"
said a Conservative, "how he is to make up the deficiency
without an additional income tax, and if he proposes that
he is done." "Well, we shall have no repeal of the paper
duty this year," said an advanced Liberal, "that's clear."
And when gradually the Chancellor unfolded his scroll, and
showed that, instead of its being written all over with
lamentations and woe, it was radiant with success in the
past and hope for the future, and that, instead of having
a deficiency to provide for, he had a surplus to distribute,
the joy of the Liberal party was unbounded, and the
astonishment of the Opposition was manifest. Long and
loud were the cheers on the Government side when the
fact was fairly brought out. Whigs and Radicals all
cheered, from the smug Whig doctrinaire who shoves his
knees into the backs of the Ministers down to the broadest
and most uncompromising Radical on the extreme right.
All were of one mind for once, and every face was radiant
with delight. But on the other side all grew dark as night.
This Budget had been looked forward to not without hope;
and ever since the opening of the Session, when it was asked
"whether anything was going to happen," the reply universally was, "We must wait for the Budget, and see how
Gladstone provides for his deficiency;" and now to see
this hoped-for dark deficiency resolve itself, as in a dissolving
view, into a golden balance in hand of some two millions was
not pleasant. But we must close. Of the speech itself we
must not speak. On the surpassing power to simplify and
even brilliantly illuminate masses of dull and intricate figures,
and the wonderful tact, and talent, and eloquence which it

displayed, we must not venture to say a word. For three hours the Chancellor of the Exchequer held the House by his enchantments, and when he sat down there was a burst of cheers so vigorous, so long, and so loud, as to prove that at all events the orator had not tired his audience.

CHAPTER XVI.

LORD ROBERT CECIL.

May 18, 1861. LORD ROBERT CECIL is a thorough-going Tory, one of the few specimens of the old genus—now almost extinct. On the whole, the noble Lord is unquestionably an able man, and when unexcited can talk reasonably well. That he can write well we all know, unless the report that it was he who wrote the severe article in the *Quarterly Review* upon Disraeli, and that he is one of the foremost contributors to the *Saturday Review*, is not true. But the noble Lord is excitable, and the bitter language in which he assailed the Chancellor of the Exchequer, though strictly within rules, was, as Sir George Grey reminded him, such as, happily, is seldom heard in the House. The noble Lord was certainly answerable for much of the passion which prevailed on this occasion ; and it really would be advisable that, before he again takes part in the debates, he should accept the counsel quietly offered by Mr. Gladstone, and "revise his vocabulary." It was whilst Lord Robert was speaking that the storm was at its height ; and we shall not soon forget the astounding roar of cheers from the Conservatives which burst out when he described the Chancellor of the Exchequer's conduct as "that of a pettifogging attorney, rather than a statesman," nor the indignant blast of groans with which it was answered.

And, now, what was the conduct of Mr. Disraeli in this extraordinary scene? Well, if the truth must be told, it was neither politic nor fortunate. The Conservative leader was, we humbly venture to think, impolitic in the first place in giving sanction to this factious opposition. A leader of a great party should always steer clear of faction, for neither reputation nor influence is to be gained in such an arena. But, if he was impolitic in sanctioning this factious contest, he was still more so in the mode in which he did it. For example, what political reason could be given for his rising to speak when the announcement of the adjournment had been made? The fight was over; the victory, such as it was, had been gained; members were on the wing; the excitement which had prevailed was rapidly subsiding, as it happily always does on such occasions amongst English gentlemen. Why should he have prolonged it? His object seemed to be to defend Lord Robert Cecil from the implied censure conveyed in the advice of Mr. Gladstone. But if this was his object he was not fortunate, for, in truth, he succeeded rather in damaging than defending; as, in his anxiety to throw his shield over the noble Lord, he unintentionally struck him a blow upon the head. For example—he began first by complimenting with singular adroitness the noble Lord " on the efficiency of his powers of expression "— a phrase which had so obviously a double meaning that it really appeared at first as if the speaker had intended, under the cover of praise, to convey sarcasm. Of course the opponents of the noble Lord saw the ambiguity of the phrase, and cheered and laughed uproariously. But, as if this was not bad enough, Mr. Disraeli went on to congratulate the noble Lord upon his debating powers, and to express a hope that " he would soon again take a part in the debates of the House in which he had so *greatly distinguished himself.*" Now, here was another most unfortunate turn of expression, for it seemed to have a double significance; not meant as such, of course, but so obvious that the Liberals seized hold of it, and again accepted the phrase with such prolonged cheers and laughter that for the space of a minute or more Disraeli was kept standing upon his legs quite unable to proceed, and, as our readers may well suppose, not in a very enviable state of mind. Indeed, it now became obvious that the great leader was fretted, and worried, and excited; for, on resuming, he turned round on Gladstone, exclaiming in a manner, to say the least of it, not dignified, " It is all very well to bully a colleague, but there is one party which he could assure the Chancellor of the Exchequer that it would be impossible to bully, and that was the English House of Commons."

CHAPTER XVII.

SPEECHES OF MR. DISRAELI AND LORD PALMERSTON ON THE DEATH OF THE PRINCE CONSORT—MR. LOWE, AS VICE-PRESIDENT OF THE COMMITTEE OF COUNCIL ON EDUCATION, INTRODUCES THE REVISED EDUCATION CODE —SIR STAFFORD NORTHCOTE.

Feb. 15, 1862. DISRAELI made a set speech upon the death of the Prince Consort, evidently got up especially for the occasion; and it was cleverly done: artistically manufactured, and dramatically delivered. Every sentence was an excellent piece of joinery—planed and polished like burnished steel; and all agreed that it was a clever speech, and praised it much. But it did not produce any marked effect on the House; for, with all its artistic construction, it lacked the Promethean fire of earnestness. We admired it, but it excited no feeling. The speech, however, was highly characteristic, for the right honourable gentleman is utterly devoid of pathos. In all his works (and we have read most of them) we do not recollect a line that touches the emotion of his hearers. He is excellent at description, though his descriptions are sometimes faulty in taste; he can set the House in a roar by his wit; he can point a sarcasm and hurl it at his opponents with damaging effect; and, at times, he can discover something of the quality of humour in his writings and speeches; but over the hearts of his hearers and readers he has no control; and whilst we laugh at his wit, are hurt by his sarcasm, are struck with his descriptive power, we still feel that there is a great separating gulf between him and the bulk of mankind. "One touch of nature makes the whole world kin." Mr. Disraeli wants that touch. It was a splendid opportunity for an orator, that Thursday night. There were for topics a beloved Prince suddenly snatched away, a widowed Queen, fatherless Princes, and a sorrowing nation for an audience; but Disraeli, though he had evidently prepared himself for the occasion, failed to use it to effect.

When Disraeli sat down Lord Palmerston rose; but he did not speak with his usual power. There was no sign of bodily feebleness. His voice was still clear and ringing as ever; but we missed the easy flow of words—especially in that part of the speech which referred to the death of the Prince—which generally marks the speeches of the noble Lord. But it is known that Lord Palmerston is not good at a panegyric. Every man has his gift. Lord Palmerston's gift is debate, and especially on foreign affairs; but still there was a marked difference between the noble Lord's speech and that of his predecessor. If there was not the reality of sorrow there was something very much like it, and the effect was apparent.

Feb. 22, 1862. To Mr. Robert Lowe belongs the honour of having delivered the dreariest speech that has been uttered in the House of Commons within the memory of the oldest member. He began to speak at half-past four o'clock, or thereabouts; he sat down when the hands of the dial had reached twenty minutes past eight. He spoke, therefore, nearly four hours. But it was not the length of the speech that was remarkable, for Gladstone has more than once spoken as long; Disraeli, in 1852, when he propounded his first Budget, and Palmerston when he defended his foreign policy in 1850, longer. It was the dreary monotony of the speech that distinguished it above all others that we ever heard. It was as monotonous as the hum of the bumble-bee or as the drone of a bagpipe. In short, the speech was a prolonged monotone of four hours' length. For an hour or more we followed that dull, monotonous sound, and we can declare that during all that time it did not vary a quarter-tone from the original key. At times the right honourable gentleman spoke somewhat louder or lower than at others, but the key was always the same; and the effect of the monotony was dreary in the extreme. Of course, listening to the speech throughout was an impossibility; nature is incapable of such a labour. When men travel through a sandy desert of miles in extent, they find it quite impossible after an hour or two to keep their attention fixed upon the route. They either fall asleep upon their horses or into a reverie upon objects and scenes far away. And so it was in the House on that Thursday night. It was an interesting subject that Mr. Lowe had to deal with, and one which had been much agitated during the recess, and so anxious were many of the members to understand it that they anticipated or postponed their dinners to hear what the Vice-President of the Education Board had to say upon this vexed question. But it soon became clear that all their resolution to listen sedulously was in vain; nothing could withstand the mesmeric influence of that dull, monotonous sound; and, after the first hour, it became evident that three-fourths of the members, though present in the body, were absent in spirit, and far away from the scene in the land of reverie or dream. "But it was an able speech," some reader may perhaps observe. To which we answer—no doubt a very able speech, showing great knowledge of the subject, cleverness in answering objections, and indications everywhere that the speaker is no common man; and we venture to think that the publication of this speech will produce a powerful impression upon the minds of the people, correcting many mistakes and clearing from the public mind many false notions—in short, a triumphantly successful speech, and one which, when the subject comes to be debated again and again, will stand, in the main, unanswered and unanswerable. But as to the manner in which it was delivered, that, we must maintain, was supremely bad; and here we cannot help remarking upon the strangeness of the fact that so accomplished and generally able a man as Mr. Lowe is should be unable to deliver a speech with anything like effect. But *poeta nascitur non fit;* and so it is with the orator, we suppose.

Still, though Mr. Lowe cannot deliver a speech except in the monotonous, colourless, dreary manner we have described, he must, if we come to think of his career, be considered a remarkable man. Just let us glance at that career. Mr. Lowe is the son of the Rev. Robert Lowe, a country clergyman. He was educated at Winchester and at University College, Oxford, where he took a first class in classics and second in mathematics. In 1842 he was called to the Bar at Lincoln's Inn, and in the same year went to Australia, and immediately on his arrival got into a lucrative practice at the colonial Bar. In 1843 he became member of the colonial Council, was elected for Sydney in 1848, and in 1850 returned to England with a fortune. In 1852 he got into Parliament for Kidderminster, and in July of the same year he gained so much credit by an able critical analysis of Disraeli's Budget that in the next year he was appointed one of the Secretaries of the old Board of Control. In 1855 he became Vice-President to the Board of Trade, and in 1859 was appointed President of the Board of Health and Vice-President of the Education Board of the Privy Council,

which offices he now holds. This is the right hon. gentleman's career. He took a high position—nearly the highest
—at college; he made a fortune in Australia in less than ten
years; he got into office here at home within a year after
he entered Parliament; and now he is high in office, and
a member of the Privy Council. And all this he has done
without the aid of family or other influence, but simply by
his own abilities. The personal appearance of Mr. Lowe is
singular. Though not an old man—fifty-one years of age—
his hair is perfectly white, and his eyebrows and lashes are
the same,whilst his eyes, which are small and deep-seated,
are pink. When he first came into the House it was said
that he was an Albino; and an old grumbling Conservative
was once heard to say, "I don't know what the House of
Commons will come to. Here, I am told, we've got an
Albanian now come amongst us; I wonder what we shall
have next—a nigger, I suppose." Mr. Lowe is not very
popular in the House; he is sarcastic, defiant in tone, and
intolerant of opposition; and there is a general suspicion in
the House that he writes for a certain morning paper, and
that occasionally he criticises in its columns with severity
the measures of his colleagues, which, as a Minister of the
Crown, he is bound to support. The suspicion may be
unfounded, but that it generally prevails is unquestionable;
indeed, it is taken to be indisputable. "Did you hear
Lowe's speech?" inquired one member of another. "No,"
was the reply; "but I read his articles upon the subject in
the *Times*."

May 17, 1862. In these sketches we have never given more
than a passing notice of Sir Stafford Northcote.
This was an omission which we now proceed to rectify,
for Sir Stafford Northcote is a rising man—means, indeed,
if the Fates be propitious, to mount to the Chancellorship

of the Exchequer, and is now sedulously climbing upwards to that bright official tableland by every available means, and as earnestly and carefully as an Alpine adventurer, with alpenstock in hand, mounts to some dizzy height which he has never reached before. Sir Stafford came first into Parliament in 1855, for the borough of Dudley, and held the seat until 1857. At the general election of that year he did not, however, again attempt Dudley. The reason probably was that Mr. Henry Brinsley Sheridan was in the field as a Radical candidate; and, though Sir Stafford had the Earl's support, he would not venture to front the people whom in formidable numbers Mr. Sheridan had gathered around him. But Sir Stafford was not long out of Parliament, for in 1858 there came a vacancy for Stamford, and the hon. Baronet found no difficulty in getting elected for that more Conservative place. Before Sir Stafford got into Parliament he was a man well known, and of some mark. He had taken a first class in classics at Oxford, he had been private secretary to Mr. Gladstone at the Board of Trade, and had publicly interested himself in educational and other cognate matters; indeed, so well was he thought of by the Conservative chiefs that they made him, in 1859, financial secretary to the Treasury. And there can be no doubt that within a certain range Sir Stafford has considerable abilities; he is, for example, a capital arithmetician, and if a man were wanted to manage a bank, or even to preside over the Bank of England, there could be no question that he would be fitted for the post. His friends say that he is a great financier, meaning thereby that he is competent to take charge of the finances of the nation as Chancellor of the Exchequer. But we doubt this; provisionally we should decide that he is not. He is clever, acute, and accurate, but in our humble opinion he is narrow of mind, incapable of taking a comprehensive view of a subject, and therefore not fitted to be Chancellor of the Exchequer. A notable writer speaks of certain fly-critics who settle on a capital or a cornice and discuss its merits, but cannot form an idea of the whole building; and this, we think, is an apt description of Sir Stafford. Like the bee, he could, no doubt, gather the honey very well, and store it cleverly and economically; but could he by judicious horticulture, as our present Chancellor of the Exchequer does, increase the produce? We imagine not. However, we shall probably be able to judge of his abilities more decisively soon; for report says he will certainly be Chancellor of the Exchequer in the next Conservative Government. As a speaker Sir Stafford is not attractive. In the first place, he does not discuss subjects in an attractive way. He is microscopically minute —wearisome—in his criticisms; he never gives utterance to enlarged sentiments; he is ever pulling to pieces and never building up, and he cannot appreciate the bold financial policy of the times. And besides all this, though he is voluble, never at a loss for words, has lately become much more cool and self-possessed than he used to be, and has taken to oratorical action, boldly looking his opponent in the face and enforcing his utterances with appropriate gesture, his voice is harsh and brassy, and his delivery monotonous. And so it comes to pass that what with the dryness of his matter, the harshness of his voice, and the monotony of his tones, though he generally commands silence, he cannot interest or even hold the House. If strangers wish to discover Sir Stafford in the House they may easily find him. He sits in close proximity to Disraeli. In stature he is short; he has a bushy swan-coloured beard, hair of the same hue, and always wears spectacles.

The honourable Baronet's speech was not a success. It was a mere repetition of what we have often had before; and as there was a visible feeling of disappointment when he rose, so were there equally visible signs of relief when he sat down. Mr. Forster followed Sir Stafford, but his interposition was not well timed, and the hon. member seemed, after he had risen, to feel this, for he did not speak by any means with his usual clearness and force. He, however, said one good thing, which was cordially cheered by the Liberal members of the House and deserves to be repeated. Sir Stafford Northcote had charged Mr. Gladstone with having produced discontent at Manchester, and to this charge Mr. Forster made the following reply:—"Nothing that the Chancellor of the Exchequer had said could make the Manchester men discontented, for they well knew that what he and his great mentor, Sir R. Peel, had done in opening up fresh supplies of food and fresh sources of employment was the one bright spot which they could look upon with pleasure in their present disastrous circumstances."

Is it worth while to dwell at length upon Gladstone's reply to Sir Stafford? We think not. Suffice it, then, to say that the Chancellor of the Exchequer had been threatened with an attack from a much more redoubtable foe. He had been led to expect another fierce onslaught from the great Caucasian pugilist himself, and had trained and armed accordingly for the fight. He felt, therefore, small difficulty in settling this little matter with his old pupil. Indeed, it was obvious from his tone and manner that he deemed it mere child's play. He was in the highest possible spirits. He played with his puny opponent as a flyfisher plays with a trout securely hooked. In short, the Chancellor *in esse* made the Chancellor *in posse* look miserably small. Surely it is indiscreet for Sir Stafford to encounter Gladstone: it may show his courage, but hardly his wisdom. It will be time enough to measure himself with one of such gigantic proportions some years hence,

when he shall have tried his hand and tested his abilities at
the Treasury.

Will there be a fight or not? This was the question
when Mr. Forster rose, and somehow—we know not how—
it got whispered about that there would be no fight.
Gladstone would answer Sir Stafford Northcote, the
Revenue Bill would pass its second reading, and all would
be over; and under this impression, as the witching time
for dinner had nearly arrived, many of the members, and
not a few strangers, bolted away. And great was their
mortification when they came to learn that they had lost
the best part of the night's performance. When the
telegraph spread the news through the clubs that Disraeli
was up several members left or hurriedly bolted their
dinners, and hastened back to the House as fast as hansoms
could bring them.

And now, what shall we say to Disraeli's marvellous
speech—surely one of the most remarkable harangues which
this clever, accomplished, but strange, incomprehensible,
inscrutable man ever delivered? Shall we condense it and
give its substance to our readers? Want of space forbids.
Shall we analyse and criticise it? We shrink from the
arduous task. Shall we point out its object and aim? This
would be altogether futile. For this speech, as to its object
and aim, was when it was delivered, and is now, an insoluble
problem—an enigma as profound as that of the Sphinx, or
as the Asian mystery which Disraeli dwells upon with such
awe in his books. All we can attempt is to photograph the
appearance of the House during the delivery of this incomprehensible oration. And this was singular, and in all its
circumstances, we believe, unique. The Conservative party,
then, during almost the whole of the two hours which
Disraeli occupied, seemed to be in a state of blank astonishment. They did not cheer; they expressed no dissent; they

appeared to be simply bewildered. Nor is this surprising.
Dissent they could hardly openly express, for the speaker
was their leader; and how could they cheer sentiments
which went directly in the teeth of all their principles and
contradicted all their traditions? The Irish Roman Catholics
who cluster below the gangway, when Disraeli discoursed
about the Pope and the French occupation of Rome, broke
forth now and then into faint applause; but it was only
faint and half-hearted, for what did he mean? Was he for
the Pope or against him? It was impossible to discover
which through that halo of words in which Disraeli, as is
his manner, cleverly contrived to envelop his thoughts.
When he spoke of "bloated armaments" and a diplomatic
conference with the French Emperor to obtain a mutual
disarming, of course the Radicals were delighted, and
applauded to the echo. But the Whigs behind the Government, like the Conservatives in their front, were silent, except
that now and then a sort of chuckling laugh broke forth, as
if they were delighted with and hoped to make political
capital out of the confusion worse confounded which the
speaker was creating. This was the scene, then, which
we had before us when the great Caucasian waved that
wonder-working wand of his over the House, and here we
must leave the matter.

"The Lord hath delivered him into my hands!" exclaimed
Cromwell in a pious ecstasy when he saw old Leslie, the
Scotch commander, descend from his heights at Berwick
and lay himself open to attack. Lord Palmerston is no
Puritan, and therefore no such pious exclamation escaped
his lips as he sat watching his opponent and noting his
strategical blunders; but he was equally alive with Old
Noll to the advantages which his foe was giving him, and
equally prepared when the time should come to pursue them
with energy and success. When Disraeli sat down the

noble Lord sprang to his feet—yes, literally so—with as much agility and briskness as if he had been forty years old instead of seventy-eight, as he is. And never did this marvellous old man speak with more life, jollity, fun, and energy than he did on that Thursday night. And how sagaciously did he seize the salient points of his opponent's studied harangue, clear them of their rhetorical mist, and turn his guns upon himself! Indeed, the speech was a triumph from beginning to end. Cheers broke forth at the conclusion of every sentence, and every now and then there were bursts of hearty laughter so loud and long-continued that the House seemed for a time more like a theatre during the performance of a broad farce than a hall of legislation. And here let it be noted that the Conservatives cheered this speech and joined in the laughter as loudly as the Liberals. Whilst Disraeli, their leader, was speaking, they were dumb; but when Lord Palmerston, the leader of their opponents, spoke, they cheered him to the echo. This is strange; but so it was. What it intimates or augurs we leave our readers to speculate upon as best they may. Some weeks back report said that Palmerston was miserably ill; and when he came to the House, and men saw his pale face, they exclaimed, "Ah! the old man is breaking up"; and we ourselves had our misgivings. But lo! he seems now to have renewed his youth, like the eagle. At all events, on Thursday night there were no signs of "breaking up."

Feb. 14, 1863. And now a word or two on the appearance of the more prominent members of the Commons' House of Parliament. "How does Lord Palmerston look?" was the question upon a hundred lips on the opening day of the Session; and as the noble Lord marched across the lobby a hundred eyes examined him keenly. For a time after he entered the House he was scarcely observed, for he entered at the back-door and glided unseen into his place, as his manner is. But soon he had to go to the bar, and then to the table, to present papers touching the Prince of Wales's marriage, and then every eye was fixed upon him. Cheers burst forth from his supporters when they saw that he walked as firmly as ever, and that to all appearance he was but little changed since he shook hands with the Speaker six months ago. Nor is it wonderful that we should be anxious about this old man's health, for he is in his seventy-ninth year, and upon his shoulders rests, it is now acknowledged, the whole framework of our party arrangements. Like Atlas, he alone holds up the structure ; and when he shall fail all will collapse and sink into temporary ruin. Well, we too have scanned closely the noble Lord, and this is our report. He looks a shade older than he did ; he does not walk quite so briskly as he did ; but there is evidently "life in the old dog yet" ; and, if any impatient young Conservatives are specu-lating to the tune of £1,200 a year upon the noble Lord's failure this Session, we believe and hope that their specula-tions will fail. Fail ! Why, the noble Lord has no thought of failing, for it was only the other day that he appeared in the hunting-field with a new scarlet coat. It is said, how-ever, that the Marquis of Lansdowne's death affected him deeply ; and some say that it has left its mark upon him. But *Flecti non frangere*—to be bent not broken—is his Lordship's heraldic motto ; and he who has seen so many of his political friends fall in battle will hardly permit him-self to be permanently depressed by the death of a comrade at the venerable age of eighty-two. All the other Ministers who have presented themselves seem to be hearty enough. Gladstone, however, has not appeared. He has been watch-ing the deathbed of a beloved brother, opposed to him in politics, but none the less beloved for that, and is now mourning his loss. Disraeli, from Session to Session, changes but slightly; but, catching a glimpse of him with the mind's eye as he was ten years ago, we discern a great change. Time has thinned his hair. Those "corkscrew curls," which were celebrated in the witty parody in the "Dialogus Horatii et Lydiæ," have disappeared, and he, too, is evidently, albeit he is only in his fifty-eighth year, passing gradually into the shadow of old age. His colleagues on the front bench of the Opposition have not shown in their strength. Sir John Pakington came in for a few minutes, and in him we have to report no change. Lord Stanley is getting fat. Mr. Cobden looks better than he has looked for several years, and his confrère, Mr. Bright, is unchanged. Mr. Alexander Kinglake looks haggard and worn, but is, perhaps, as "well as can be expected" so soon after the birth of that tremendous book which he has just given to the world.

END OF VOL. I.